BEYOND
INTEGRATION?

Foreword by **John Wilson,** Editor, *Books and Culture*

BEYOND INTEGRATION?

Inter/Disciplinary Possibilities

for the Future of

Christian Higher Education

Todd C. **Ream**

Jerry **Pattengale**

David L. **Riggs**

editors

Abilene Christian University Press

BEYOND INTEGRATION?
Inter/Disciplinary Possibilities for the Future of Christian Higher Education

ACU
PRESS

Copyright 2012 by ACU Press

ISBN 978-0-89112-317-0
LCCN 2012002324

Printed in the United States of America

Scripture quotations noted NRSV are taken from the Revised Standard Version of the Bible, copyright 1952 [2nd edition, 1971] by the Division of Christian Education of the National Council of the Churches of Christ in the United States of America. Used by permission. All rights reserved.

LIBRARY OF CONGRESS CATALOGING-IN-PUBLICATION DATA
Beyond integration : inter/disciplinary possibilities for the future of Christian higher education / Todd C. Ream, Jerry Pattengale, and David L. Riggs, editors ; foreword by John Wilson.
    p. cm.
Includes index.
ISBN 978-0-89112-317-0
1. Christian universities and colleges--United States. 2. Christian education--United States. 3. Interdisciplinary approach in education--United States. I. Ream, Todd C. II. Pattengale, Jerry A. III. Riggs, David L. (David Lee), 1967-
LC427.B49 2012
378'.071--dc23
                                                                2012002324

Cover design by Rick Gibson
Interior text design by Sandy Armstrong

The cover photo is of the Williams Prayer Chapel and Jackson Library on the campus of Indiana Wesleyan University. Used by permission.

For information contact:
Abilene Christian University Press
1626 Campus Court
Abilene, Texas 79601

1-877-816-4455
www.abilenechristianuniversitypress.com

12 13 14 15 16 17 / 7 6 5 4 3 2 1

To the Students of Indiana Wesleyan University's

John Wesley Honors College

May They Benefit from the Wisdom Found in these Pages

in Ways Comparable to the Wisdom They Shared with Us

TABLE OF CONTENTS

FOREWORD

John Wilson

The fine essays collected in this volume remind me of a recurring scenario in the science fiction of the 1950s. Imagine a vast assembly hall where ambassadors of far-flung interstellar realms are gathered to deal with some impending crisis. These dignitaries don't merely speak different languages—they represent a multiplicity of species, adapted to radically different living conditions. And, in some instances at least, they are divided by ancient enmities. (What you have is a cross between the United Nations and the cantina scene from *Star Wars*). How can they possibly work together for the common good? Is there even a common good to be found?

At first glance, such a scenario would seem to have no bearing on the virtual conclave made possible by this book. After all, the authors speak the same language and work in the same environment: the academy. Most important, all of them write from a robustly Christian perspective. And the problem they are addressing—how we should frame the relationship between faith and learning, with an emphasis on interdisciplinary approaches—hardly seems analogous to a crisis sufficiently urgent to provoke a special session of the Galactic General Assembly.

On closer inspection, though, there are some noteworthy similarities. Let's start with the sense of urgency. In its centenary year, 2011, Eerdmans published Mark Noll's book *Jesus Christ and the Life of the Mind,* which is—among other things—a sequel of sorts to his 1994 book *The Scandal of the Evangelical Mind*. At the end of the new book, we find this resonant paragraph:

> If, as Christians believe, "all the treasures of wisdom and knowledge" are hid in Christ (Col. 2:3), the time is always past for talking about treasure hunting. The time is always now to unearth treasure, offer it to others for critique and affirmation, and above all to find in it new occasions to glorify the one who gives the treasure and is the treasure himself.

The time is always now—meaning *now*, right now, as you are reading these words. As Noll warns, this sense of urgency isn't a warrant for unconsidered action (as it all too often has been in evangelical circles). "Be quick but don't hurry," John Wooden told his players at UCLA. But it does remind us that this collection of essays is not "academic" in the pejorative sense: narrow, of coterie interest only. On the contrary.

So here we have a gathering of experts called, in their own way, to address the very subject of Noll's book: Jesus Christ and the life of the mind. Each writer represents a particular discipline. And we might expect to collate their reports to get a reasonably adequate Big Picture.

But there's a problem. I said earlier that—unlike the delegates at the galactic assembly—all of the contributors to this volume speak the same language. Technically, that's true. But many different Englishes appear in this book, and it wouldn't be an exaggeration to say that each discipline has its own language. In fact, each discipline (seen in a certain aspect) is its own species. The sociologist might be the equivalent of the galactic delegate who resembles a gigantic praying mantis, while the philosopher might be the counterpart of the green-skinned humanoid delegate with the enormous, unblinking eyes. Although all of the contributors live and work in the academy, their essays—overlapping at some points, contradicting one another elsewhere, and often proceeding on separate tracks—can't readily be assembled to form a coherent picture.

Is this the fault of the contributors? The editors? Does it negate the argument for interdisciplinary approaches on which the volume is premised? To all three questions, the answer is no.

To get the right answers, we need to step back and think about this particular moment. We are emerging from a period in which—under a banner announcing the end of "metanarratives," the exhaustion of grand theories, and so on and so on, *ad nauseum*—many scholars have been promulgating a metanarrative so meta, it has threatened to swallow up everything in its path. According to this metanarrative, a vast conspiracy known as "modernity" led us astray for a few centuries. (Cue the image of Descartes, Kant, and John Nelson Darby, wearing masks like the Beagle Boys.) Then . . . but you know how the rest of the story goes; no need to spell it out here.

Fortunately, most of the juice seems to be gone from this line of argument. Both its ardent defenders and its fierce critics appear to be worn out, though they continue to go through the motions. Perhaps it's not too fanciful, then, to hope for an interregnum during which scholars will pay attention to the irreducible claims of different ways of understanding the world—precisely such as are represented by the essays in this volume (and including those that continue to make use of the mother of all metanarratives).

"Some forms of pluralism," wrote Elizabeth Fox-Genovese and Hugh Kenner early in the history of the idiosyncratic journal *Common Knowledge*, "are based upon tolerance of or interest in viewpoints not one's own, some forms on shallow understanding of the term 'viewpoint,' other forms on *folie de doute*." In contrast, Fox-Genovese and Kenner called for arguments that "discredit pluralism—the mere tolerance of multiple viewpoints—in favor of [an] approach, founded in non-foundational philosophy, that renders every internally coherent viewpoint *indispensable*."

Both Fox-Genovese (late in life) and Kenner (as a young man) were converts to Catholicism. They were confident, as all Christians should be, in the coherence of the world, and it was this confidence that permitted them to claim that the "best response to an inquiry about anything is . . . everything" (ellipses theirs). As "overdeterminists," they argued that, while "no circumstance can be arbitrary," nevertheless "the determinants of any given circumstance are unlimited; hence, to some degree, unknowable." And that is why, again, they called for an approach "that renders every internally coherent viewpoint *indispensable*."

What we have in this volume is a gathering of reports on the current state of the conversation about faith and learning. Each report does two things. Explicitly, it describes the situation as it appears from the perspective of a particular discipline. Implicitly, by virtue of its appearance in this collection, and sometimes explicitly as well, each essay simultaneously calls for attention to the reports issued from other disciplines.

Are we to regard the organization of knowledge in the early twenty-first-century university as timeless? Certainly not. But we should be wary of attempts to write obituaries for the disciplines in the name of some higher—and cooler—truth. Better to carry on conversations in which both the commonalities and the differences among different modes of understanding are given their due.

Which takes us back to that sci-fi scenario from the 1950s. In one version, the story played out to a peaceful resolution. On an imagined galactic stage, the hopes of the recently founded United Nations were fulfilled. But in another version, conflict was resolved—insofar as it ever could be, the various authors hinted—only by a battle to the death.

The essays gathered here remind us—in case we've somehow forgotten—that reflection among twenty-first-century Western Christians on the relationship between faith and learning takes place in a context where the dominant powers in the academy are largely if not entirely hostile to such reflection. On this subject as on many others, the essayists arrive at no consensus.

Perhaps we should be thankful for that, and not only because it suggests an occasion for a sequel to this volume. We can hold in our minds, on the one hand, an image of the many-sided universe, creation diverse beyond our comprehension, encompassing the Martian sandworm and the dirigible behemothaur and much else exceeding the limits of the little planet we call home; and on the other hand, an image of conflict between fundamentally opposing visions of our common reality: right and wrong. We need both images, even if (this side of glory) we can't entirely grasp how they fit together.

INTRODUCTION

Todd C. Ream, Jerry Pattengale, and David L. Riggs

In *Conceiving the Christian College,* former Wheaton College President Duane Litfin offers that the phrase the "integration of faith and learning" "represents the best shorthand description of what Christian colleges and universities are about."[1] At their core, these institutions are called to offer an understanding of how all forms of learning fall under the lordship of Jesus Christ. However, Litfin also suggests that many of us who serve as faculty members and administrators at these institutions are beginning to ask "whether we may be losing our grasp on what this venerable slogan was designed to convey."[2]

On the surface, this assertion by Litfin seems difficult to accept. Over the course of the last twenty-five years, Christian colleges and universities witnessed unprecedented quantitative and qualitative growth. Despite the challenges which began with the financial recession of 2008, many of these schools are now much larger and much better resourced than they were a quarter century ago. In general, the faculty members serving these institutions are academically better prepared than their predecessors and are also more heavily invested in their respective disciplines (or interdisciplinary areas of inquiry). Several centers dedicated to supporting the interplay between faith and learning have emerged in recent years and many tenure committees at these schools now even require candidates for promotion to submit integration papers as part of their portfolios.

Perhaps one part of this dilemma that Litfin references came as a result of the success that the "integration of faith and learning" has enjoyed.[3] With its origins residing in the philosophical and theological insights of the Reformed tradition, this phrase has now expanded its influence to institutions nurtured by any number of Christian traditions.[4] Initially, several schools in the Arminian or holiness traditions adopted this phrase as part of the vernacular spoken and practiced on their campuses. However, in *Scholarship and Christian Faith: Enlarging the Conversation*, Douglas Jacobsen and Rhonda Hustedt Jacobsen contend that "they will move beyond the integration approach to explore the broader world of Christian scholarship which encompasses many different ways of reflecting on faith and learning."[5] Reflecting the Arminian ethos of Messiah College, the chapters in their text include a panoply of options concerning the changing nature of the relationship shared by faith and learning.

Perhaps another part of this dilemma comes with the erosion of barriers once separating the academic disciplines.[6] Lines of demarcation between disciplines as different as philosophy and physics are proving to be less distinguishable—particularly if one compares them with the lines in place just thirty years ago.[7] Risking oversimplification, the integration of faith and learning was initially defined by the bringing together of various theological principles and the content from a singular academic discipline; the result can be seen, for example, in the CCCU's joint effort with HarperCollins in publishing the "Through the Eyes of Faith" series. How does this process now take place when scholars are currently pursuing work at the intersections of or even between any number of disciplines?

Compounding this challenge are a growing number of voices who contend that to insist upon theology as being an academic discipline is to reduce it to being just another form of knowledge. In contrast, these scholars want to see a return of theology to its place as the "Queen of the Sciences." The integration of faith and learning becomes a practice to continue if we are no longer talking about drawing together distinct disciplines. Perhaps one could thus surmise that the integration of faith and learning was stretched beyond the context of its original theological tradition at the same time that academe was beginning to ponder life beyond these previously prescribed academic boundaries. Theological traditions beyond the Reformed movement became invested in this practice at the same time disciplinary boundaries began eroding.

The purpose of this volume is to draw together a number of prominent voices who are beginning to reflect upon the nature of Christian scholarship as it may exist beyond the influence of the integration model. In particular, they consider what moving beyond the integration model might mean for shaping and theoretically framing curricula. If the original design of the integration model is now beginning to demonstrate its limits (even if those limits emerged as a result of this model's own success), what is emerging in its place?

In addition, the contributors to this volume also think through how such forms of speculation about the future of the integration model are impacted by eroding disciplinary lines. While the contributors are steeped in the practices of their particular discipline (including John W. Wright who is a theologian), they also share a keen interest in understanding how their discipline is being shaped and re-shaped by changes in other disciplines. For example, John Schmalzbauer's contribution concerning sociology is just as influenced by practices in history, theology, and philosophy as his own field. In essence, his remarks, like many of the others included in this volume, pose serious questions about where the lines of demarcation between the disciplines now begin and end or even if such lines exist anymore—especially for the Christian scholar.

In order to contend with this reality and thus the awkward question of how to shape this book, we limited its focus to individuals who represent the highest ideals of Christian scholarship in areas historically thought to comprise the core of an undergraduate general education curriculum—the natural sciences, the social sciences, the behavioral sciences, and the liberal arts. Contributors include scholars who have emerged as seminal voices in their respective fields (however those fields are now defined) and have wrestled with some of the larger questions facing Christian academe.

For example, David Lyle Jeffrey and Mary Stewart Van Leeuwen are among a generation of scholars who paved the way for numerous opportunities in regard to the integration of faith and learning that now benefit the emerging generation of scholars. Edward B. Davis, Timothy

Larsen, Jeanne Heffernan Schindler, John A. Schmalzbauer, James K. A. Smith, and John W. Wright have now joined the ranks of scholars such as David and Mary. In an emerging scholar such as Jade Avelis, we see a bright future as she and her classmates at places such as Notre Dame are wrestling with questions not only at the forefront of their fields but the nature of knowledge as a whole.

Most of the contributions in this volume were originally delivered as lectures at Indiana Wesleyan University as part of the Athens and Jerusalem Forum series. Through this ongoing series, faculty members across the university are given the opportunity to read through a text of great promise concerning the nature of Christian scholarship. After the conclusion of these reading groups, the author of the respective text visits the campus and makes a public address. These reading groups and lectures have proven to be ways of injecting hope, breadth, and depth into the scholarship and pedagogy of faculty members at Indiana Wesleyan.

In addition to heartfelt thanks to each one of these contributors, we extend appreciation to the Lilly Endowment and the funding it provided in the spring of 2005 to Indiana Wesleyan through its Intellectual Capital Initiative. In an attempt to recruit and retain the brightest scholarly minds to the state of Indiana, this initiative has given the Indiana Wesleyan University community the opportunity to interact with the array of prominent scholars represented in these pages. We expect the fruit of that initiative to continue for years and be seen in both the quality and quantity of scholarly opportunities dotting our campus.

A special word of appreciation is also due to our provost, David W. Wright, and our president, Henry L. Smith. The two of them have come together in an attempt to inspire the highest standards of scholarship and teaching—standards that bear witness to the redemptive power of the Christian narrative. In just a few short years, they have helped us think through, in new and exciting ways, what it means to be a Christ-centered academic community.

Finally, we wish to offer a special word of appreciation to the students who make the John Wesley Honors College such a unique place to serve. Their energy, intellectual capabilities, and passion for the transformative power of the gospel is a blessing which makes our callings as teachers rewarding in ways that defy description. Many of them heard the words included in these pages in their original forms and were inspired to think anew about their own vocations. Each spring we watch another class of students graduate—a moment of mixed emotions of pride over their achievements and grief over the fact that we will no longer share in one another's immediate company on a daily basis. Our hope is that they benefit from the wisdom found in these pages in ways comparable to the wisdom they shared with us.

Greentown & Marion, Indiana
Ecclesiastical New Year, 2011

Introduction Notes

1. Duane Litfin, *Conceiving the Christian College* (Grand Rapids, MI: Eerdmans, 2004), 127.

2. Ibid.

3. See Douglas Jacobsen and Rhonda Hustedt Jacobsen, *Scholarship and Christian Faith: Enlarging the Conversation* (New York, NY: Oxford University Press, 2004).

4. The most influential works offered by adherents to the Reformed tradition include books by Arthur Holmes, George Marsden, and Nicholas Wolterstorff, to name only a few.

5. Jacobsen and Jacobsen, *Scholarship and Christian Faith*, p. 16.

6. Whether or not they employ the language of integration, several volumes (in whole or in part) look at the practice of scholarship in relation to the disciplines. See Michael L. Budde and John Wright, eds., *Conflicting Allegiances: The Church-Based University in a Liberal Democratic Society* (Grand Rapids, MI: Brazos Press, 2004); David Claerbaut, *Faith and Learning on the Edge* (Grand Rapids, MI: Zondervan, 2004); Harold Heie and David L. Wolfe, eds., *The Reality of Christian Learning: Strategies for Faith-Discipline Integration* (Eugene, OR: Wipf and Stock, 2004); Arlin C. Migliazzo, ed., *Teaching as an Act of Faith: Theory and Practice in Church-Related Higher Education* (New York, NY: Fordham University Press, 2002); and Andrea Sterk, ed., *Religion, Scholarship, and Higher Education: Perspectives, Models, and Future Prospects* (Notre Dame, IN: University of Notre Dame Press, 2002).

7. See Michael Peters, ed., *After the Disciplines: The Emergence of Cultural Studies* (Westport, CT: Bergin and Garvey, 1999), for a discussion of the changing nature of the academic disciplines.

BEYOND INTEGRATION

Re-Narrating Christian Scholarship in Postmodernity

James K. A. Smith

Introduction: The Project of "the Christian College"

One of the most interesting aspects of the CCCU network of Christian colleges over the past decade or so has been the increased and almost ubiquitous conviction that a "Christian" college is not just an institution that provides daily worship and a sanctified atmosphere in the dorms. Rather, it seems to be a settled conviction that the Christian-ness of the institution should inform the educational and academic project that is the central task of a college. What makes the college "Christian" is not (just) the chapel, but the curriculum. And in particular, a Christian curriculum is one informed by a Christian "worldview." Thus we have seen an explosion of literature on worldviews and the "integration" of faith and learning across the disciplines.

I want to register some reservations with the "integration" project—not in the name of rejecting the project of "Christian scholarship," but rather in the name of a more radical understanding of Christian scholarship.[1] I want to invite us to consider the shape of Christian scholarship beyond "integration" and after "worldview." As part of this project, I will suggest that postmodernism—and specifically the postmodern critique of Enlightenment models of rationality (and hence the received standards of "scholarship" and "theory")—is an important catalyst for developing a more radical vision of Christian scholarship, one that I'll describe as "*un*apologetics." To do this, I first want to articulate a critique of "worldview"-talk and "integration"-talk as they have been adopted (and adapted) in discussions of Christian scholarship and Christian higher education. Second, I want to show how philosophical reflection can serve the project of Christian scholarship by discerning the problems with the *status quo*. In particular, I will argue that the postmodern critique of Enlightenment rationality—and the "thinking-thing-*ism*" that attends it—should push us to stop talking about worldviews and instead focus on what Charles Taylor describes as "the social imaginary." The same should also push us to stop talking about "integration" and instead develop a more radical model of Christian scholarship I'll describe as *un*apologetics. Then, in the final section, I will suggest that a focus on the Christian social imaginary should re-invigorate a role for Scripture and worship in the project of Christian scholarship and Christian higher education.

I. The Trouble with "Worldview," or the Ghosts of Descartes and Kant in Christian Higher Education

A. "Thinking-thing-ism" and the Distortion of "Worldview"

Many Christian colleges and universities—particularly in the Protestant tradition—have taken on board a picture of the human person that owes more to modernity and the Enlightenment than it does to the holistic, biblical vision of human persons.[2] In particular, Christian education has absorbed a philosophical anthropology that sees human persons as primarily thinking things. The result has been an understanding of education largely in terms of *in*formation rather than formation; more specifically, the end of Christian education has been seen to be the dissemination and communication of Christian *ideas* rather than the formation of a peculiar people. This can be seen most acutely, I think, in how visions of Christian education have been articulated in terms of a Christian "worldview."

Over the past couple of decades, the growth of Christian colleges and universities has been attended by expanded discussions of their mission as "the integration of faith and learning." It is then commonly claimed that students at Christian colleges and universities will learn a "Christian worldview"; or they will learn what everyone else learns but "from a Christian perspective" or a "Christian point of view." Christian scholarship is taken to be scholarship informed by a Christian worldview, or scholarship that offers a "Christian perspective" on X, Y, or Z. Increasingly in these conversations, however, "a Christian worldview" is identified primarily as a set of doctrines or a system of beliefs—the sorts of statements and propositional claims that can be bullet-pointed on a PowerPoint presentation. Consider, for instance, Francis Beckwith's definition of "worldview" in a recent collection:

> What we mean is that the Christian faith is a philosophical tapestry of interdependent ideas, principles and metaphysical claims that are derived from the Hebrew-Christian Scriptures as well as the creeds, theologies, communities, ethical norms and institutions that have flourished under the authority of these writings. These beliefs are not mere utterances of private religious devotion but are propositions whose proponents claim accurately instruct us on the nature of the universe, human persons, our relationship with God, human communities and the moral life.[3]

This is echoed in more popular usage of the notion of "worldview" that advocates "thinking 'worldview-ishly'" and the importance of "worldview-thinking" by putting the Christian "belief-system" at the center of our cognition because "how a person *thinks* significantly influences his [*sic*] *actions*."[4] Kenneth Samples, like others, sees worldviews primarily as *theoretical* systems, though they often remain implicit and unarticulated. But even when implicit he construes them as still primarily cognitive. Thus, when he discusses the major components of a worldview, he suggests each worldview includes a metaphysics, an epistemology, an axiology, and more. A worldview is a set of implicit *ideas*. I'm going to suggest that this is a category mistake that indicates a reductionistic, rationalistic, dualistic anthropology (or model of the human person).

Such construals of "worldview" belie an understanding of Christian faith that is dualistic and thus reductionistic: it reduces Christian faith primarily to a set of "ideas," "principles," "claims," and "propositions" which are "known" and "believed." The goal of all this is "correct" thinking. This makes it sound as if we are essentially the sorts of things that Descartes described us to be: thinkers with ideas. But what if that is actually only a small slice of who we are? And what if, in fact, that's not even the most important part? There's also more going on in such notions of a Christian worldview: we are not only reduced to primarily thinking things, we are also seen as things whose bodies are non-essential (and rather regrettable) containers for our "minds"—as if we were really just brains-on-a-stick. This is why such construals of a Christian "worldview" are also dualistic: they tend to assume a distinction between our "souls" and our "bodies," and then tend to ignore our embodiment (or wish it weren't there). But what if our bodies are essential to our identities? Weren't we created *as* embodied creatures? What if the core of our identity is "located" more in the body than the mind?

It is this sort of rendition of "worldview" that has been adopted as an orienting concept by Christian colleges and universities from a range of Christian traditions and theological sensibilities. However, at just the time when "worldview" has come to enjoy a wide consensus among such institutions, it seems that the concept has been subject to widespread distortion and misappropriation. In particular, earlier articulations of "worldview" emerged largely from the Reformed tradition that traced a line to Abraham Kuyper who, in his famous Stone Lectures at Princeton, advocated the distinctives of Calvinism as a "world- and life-view."[5] But within this Reformed articulation, the notion of "worldview" referred to pre-rational, pre-cognitive lived-commitments that were more "existential" than cognitive.[6] In fact, the Reformational notion of "worldview" was actually meant to counter a dualistic rationalism that wanted to reduce Christian faith to a set of intellectual claims and propositions—exactly what is now being purveyed under the banner of "worldview"![7] But given that most recently the term "worldview" has been co-opted to name just such a rationalist, individualist, abstract, dis-embodied, "talking-head" kind of Christianity, I would like to call for (at least) a temporary moratorium on the use of "worldview" as a way of articulating the end (goal) of Christian education or the task of Christian scholarship. In fact, I would like to suggest a general moratorium on the sloppy shorthand of "worldview" talk because it has reduced Christian faith to a system of beliefs and propositions—and it does so because it has assumed a stunted picture of human persons as primarily thinking things.

In contrast, drawing on a philosophical anthropology that sees humans as primarily *desiring* creatures and *liturgical* animals, I want to suggest that "the Christian worldview" is not a system of propositions recorded in "statements of faith"; rather, Christian faith is primarily a narrative that is embedded and embodied in the practices of Christian worship.[8] Being a disciple of Jesus is not primarily a matter of getting the right ideas and doctrines and beliefs into your head in order to guarantee proper "behavior"[9]; rather, it's a matter of being the kind of person who *loves* rightly—who loves God and neighbor and is oriented to the world by the primacy of that love. We are made to be such people by our immersion in the material practices of Christian worship—through affective impact over time of sights and smell in water and wine. The liturgy is a pedagogy that trains us as disciples precisely by putting our bodies through a regimen for repeated practices that get hold of our heart and "aim" our love toward the kingdom of God. Before we articulate a "worldview," we worship. Before we put into words the lineaments of an ontology or an epistemology, we pray for God's healing and illumination. Before we theorize the nature of God, we sing his praises. Before we express moral principles, we receive forgiveness. Before we codify the doctrine of Christ's two natures, we receive the body of Christ in the Eucharist. Before we think, we pray. That's the kind of animals we are, first and foremost: loving, desiring, affective, liturgical animals who, for the most part, don't inhabit the world as thinkers or cognitive machines. My contention is that, given the sort of animals we are, we pray *before* we believe, we worship *before* we "know"—and that should make a difference for how we conceive the project of Christian scholarship and Christian education.

B. *"Integration," Secularity, and the Challenge of Syncretism*
If "worldview"-talk tends to assume a lingering modernist anthropology, I think "integration"-talk tends to assume a lingering, modernist epistemology that prizes "objectivity." The "integration" project is often beset

by an internal tension that threatens implosion: on the one hand, the integration project rejects the "secularist" orthodoxy of the academy and seeks to develop distinctively *Christian* scholarship; on the other hand, the project assumes a certain "givenness" in the supposed "objectivity" of the sciences. But it is just this myth of objectivity that underwrites the scruples of secularity.[10] The result, I would suggest, is a kind of Christian scholarship that is actually a mode of syncretism.

Consider a familiar passage of Scripture, one from Colossians often quoted to me by well-meaning pastors and brothers and sisters in Christ concerned about my faith as a philosopher: *"See to it that no one takes you captive through philosophy and empty deception, according to the tradition of men, according to the elementary principles of the world, rather than according to Christ"* (Col. 2:8). One of the primary challenges in Colossae was a kind of syncretism: a notion that one could simply add Christ to existing structures and commitments. One could describe this as a sanctification strategy: one takes existing cultural products and then sanctifies or "redeems" them by "adding" Jesus (a formula readily illustrated in CCM music where one simply adopts the current paradigms of pop music and then interjects lyrics that ramp up the JPMs, "Jesuses-per-minute"). Unfortunately, all too often talk of "integrating" faith and learning tends to adopt a similar Colossian strategy. Such syncretism, I think, is one of the fundamental temptations of Christian scholarship (and the arts, too): to suppose that we can take up existing theoretical frameworks and "sanctify" them in some way by mere *addition*. Such a strategy produces several less-than-integral modes of Christian scholarship and comes in several forms:

1. The first is what I would call *moralizing* Christian scholarship. In this model what distinguishes *Christian* scholarship is not our theoretical commitments *per se*, but rather the way we practice our discipline. Christian scholars will be honest, virtuous, and concerned with justice, etc. Here the Christian scholars end up being the ones doing "ethics" in their field. But even then, the "ethics" articulated seems to be little touched by the particularities of Christian

commitments. Instead it traffics in more generic (supposedly "universal") categories and concepts.[11]

2. The second is what we might describe as *topical* Christian scholarship. Here we employ the standard or "accepted" theoretical frameworks of our field (what Kuhn would call the paradigms of "normal science"), but because we're Christians, we turn these tools toward "religious topics." So Christian historians work on the history of religion in America (rather than, say, the history of Marxism in China), or Christian philosophers work on the existence of God and the problem of evil (rather than the ontology of categories or something less "religious"), or Christian directors produce and direct religious-themed plays, or Christian engineers work on "mission" development. In all of these cases, the Christian scholars adopt the same theoretical frameworks and paradigms of supposedly "objective" reason without much question. They just use these tools on different ("religious") projects.

3. A third kind of Christian scholarship that I would suggest is problematic is what I would call *theistic* scholarship. (One of my colleagues at Calvin likes to talk about "methodological theism.") Now, this might seem like hair-splitting, but let me put this as starkly as possible, in terms we might describe as Pascalian: I do not believe that "theistic" scholarship is *Christian*.[12] If theism is merely committed to something like a belief in the existence of God—even if in a very classical sense—that is not, in my book, Christianity. And thus what one gets in the name of "theistic" scholarship are broad appeals to values or "natural law" or "the image of God" or creation or justice. But it fails to speak of the cross, the resurrection, or the coming kingdom. The God of theism, to paraphrase Pascal, is not the God of Abraham or the Father of Jesus Christ. How "Christian" could our vision of Christian scholarship be if the cross and the church never show up?

I think these models (moral, topical, theistic) are newer versions of the Colossian problem; in other words, they are not sufficiently *radical*. By that I mean that these models of Christian scholarship do not interrogate the very paradigms that govern the shape of theory and scholarship in the academy. They don't question the *roots* (*radix*) from which these paradigms grow—the pre-scientific and pre-theoretical assumptions that govern the paradigms of "normal science" in the various disciplines. Instead, they simply assume the objectivity of the disciplines as disclosing "the way things are," and then seek somehow to connect Christian themes or interests with the regnant paradigms in the field. These models of "integration" are really just models of *correlation*: they cede the "truth" of a particular sphere (say, economics or linguistics or psychology) to the disclosures of a purportedly neutral, objective "science"—and then seek to correlate Christian themes and interests with the field as defined by "secular" science.[13]

When I say that correlationist models of Christian scholarship are insufficiently *radical*, I'm invoking a metaphor of *roots* (Latin: *radix*). If we try to tease this out with the metaphor, we could say that correlationist models of Christian scholarship ("integration" models) are *grafting* projects: they seek to graft Christian concerns, interests, and topics onto the plant of scholarship that grows from the roots of regnant paradigms in the field. They're trying to add Christian branches to the tree of the academy. This is because correlationism takes the existing roots as *givens* within a particular discipline—as if there's only one plant, only one root. And this is precisely the story that many of the disciplines would have us believe: there's only one "normal science," loaded with a "constellation of beliefs" (Kuhn) and assumptions about the nature of the world, the nature of knowledge, and so forth. Anything that is going to count as "scholarship" has to be grafted onto this one root. According to this model, Christian scholarship will be a matter of grafting branches onto the existing tree. Or, in terms of the Colossian problem, Christian scholarship is a matter of *addition*. (We'll return to this metaphor below.)

To use slightly different categories, we could say that such correlationist models of "integration" fail to call into question a foundationalist account of Reason of the sort bequeathed to us by the Enlightenment:

the notion of a capital-R Reason as universal, objective, neutral, and secular, and thus untainted by the particularities of bias, prejudice, or presuppositions.[14] On this account, to be "rational" is to overcome the "immaturity" of belief and tradition and to emerge into the public sphere of impartial reasoned discourse and cold, hard "facts."[15] This is the vision of rationality that, for the most part, is inscribed in us by our graduate school formation. The price of admission to the halls of the academy is the requirement that one leave one's tradition and presuppositions at the door.[16] This is why there is an intimate and inextricable link between foundationalism and secularism. Foundationalist accounts of rationality are trenchantly anti-pluralist: there is only one "right" way to know, only one mode of Reason—a mode that eschews the influence of tradition, faith, or other "influences." The space of rational discourse—whether the academy or the "public"—is thus taken to be fundamentally monolithic. For all the talk of pluralism and multiculturalism, the secularist project of the academy is remarkably Babelian in its desire to impose "one tongue" upon all who would speak otherwise.

And yet at the same time we have a strong sense that our faith matters to our scholarship. Indeed, we're all here because we teach at Christian colleges that see faith as integral to the academic project. And yet we can't quite shake this vision of "rationality." The result is the sort of correlationist projects I've sketched so far, which try somehow to "supplement" the existing paradigms by "adding" Christian faith in various ways.

II. Postmodernism and a Project for "Radical" Christian Scholarship

A. Beyond Integration: Postmodernism and a Biblical Vision of "Knowledge"

Now, why should that be a problem? Wouldn't the alternative be to give up on the academic project and retreat into some kind of fundamentalist enclave—eschewing reason and retreating into a fortress of faith? Or giving up on the whole notion of "Christian" scholarship?

I want to suggest that there is a third way here—which is not middle of the road. In order to sketch this, let me try to unpack what I think is wrong with the "correlationist" models above (and perhaps talk of "integration" in general). The correlationist or integration project operates on the basis of a model of Reason and rationality which I think is well lost and rightly criticized. The notion of an objective, neutral, unbiased "secular" reason has been roundly criticized over the past century— from Kuyper to Derrida (with Heidegger, Gadamer, Foucault, and MacIntyre in between). In sum, I think the correlationist project has failed to appreciate the postmodern critique of Enlightenment accounts of "rationality." It has bought the story that the dominant "root" is the only root in town. Or, to put this more starkly, the correlationist vision of "integration" is a thoroughly *modern* project and, as such, is a passenger on a sinking ship.

But why should Christians have any truck with postmodernism? Shouldn't our commitment to the task of "integration" lead us to stand up in defense of modernity and rationality against the wily criticisms of postmodernism? Shouldn't Christian scholars above all be committed to defending "objective reason" against the fiery darts of postmodernists?

No. In short, no. I have argued extensively elsewhere[17] that Christian scholars should find an *ally*, not an enemy, in the postmodern critique of Enlightenment rationality. Not because Christians should be "hip," "with it," and *avant garde*, but because the postmodern critique of "objective" reason actually echoes the *biblical* critique of supposedly autonomous rationality.[18] In particular, there are three themes of the "postmodern" or "postliberal" critique of secular reason which resonate with the biblical narrative:

1. *Finitude*: Heidegger and his heirs emphasized that as finite creatures we ineluctably "see" the world on the basis of presuppositions and perspectives that are a feature of our being located in time and space. We can never have the sort of disembodied, universal, objective "God's-eye-view" promised to us by the Enlightenment (something feminist scholars have also pointed out). In the same way, Scripture emphasizes that we are created as temporal, embodied, finite creatures—and that's a *good* thing (Gen. 1:31). So the conditions of finitude—which are the conditions of

creaturehood—are affirmed as something good, not a curse.[19]

2. *Tradition*: One of the key features of our finitude and embodiment is our ineluctable relationality. We are created as social animals and, as such, we inherit from others ways of being in the world. This "handing down" of possibilities and perspectives is what Gadamer and MacIntyre emphasize in their account of tradition, and it resonates with both biblical and ecclesiastical tradition.[20]

3. *Noetic effects of sin*: The biblical picture rejects the notion of a universal "objective" reason primarily because it emphasizes that sin affects not just our "moral" behavior but also our epistemic capacities (Rom. 1:18-31; 1 Cor. 2:1-5). This is often described as the "noetic effects of sin" which indicates the way in which sin affects our perception and interpretation of phenomena. The correlate is, for instance, Paul's emphasis on the illumination that is required in order for one to "see rightly." By emphasizing the role and effect of these "background conditions," the Scriptures exhibit an "epistemology" that has no room for Enlightenment confidence in "objective" rationality.[21]

The point I want to emphasize here is that there is a resonance between the postmodern critique of foundationalism or "objective" reason and the biblical account of the situatedness and conditioning of our "knowledge." I'm not saying that Christians should be postmodern for the sake of being postmodern; rather, I'm suggesting that Christian scholars find in postmodernism a catalyst for retrieving a more radical—and perhaps more biblical—account of rationality.

If we follow through on this postmodern/biblical account of reason and knowledge, then I think we are in a place to sketch a more radical account of Christian scholarship—scholarship which works from *roots* (theoretical commitments) which are integrally Christian.[22] But what this requires is a rejection of the secularism of the academy, along with its undergirding foundationalism. Christian scholars, in other words, should be decidedly on the side of pluralism.[23] To return to our botanical metaphor, Christian scholars should refuse to buy the story that there is only one root in town. In short, we should reject the secularist story that tells us that the academy (or a particular discipline) has only one plant, and therefore only one root. The postmodern critique of foundationalism shows us that the academy is a *garden*—a collection of different roots, a space of multiple (and competing) paradigms. Integral, unapologetic scholarship can flourish only insofar as we reject the monolithic and hegemonic secularism of foundationalist accounts of Reason, and instead appreciate that the academy—and scholarship—is a contested, *pluralist* space. Thus Christian scholarship, like Yahweh in Genesis 11, should be on the side of pluralism.[24] Let many flowers bloom![25]

The postmodern critique of foundationalism articulates the way in which *every* scholar is a *confessional* scholar. What counts as evidence, what counts as rational, what counts as knowledge are all tethered to pre-theoretical assumptions, stories, traditions, and beliefs that govern theory. All scholarship is theory-laden and all theory is faith-laden. And while I am describing this critique of foundationalism as "postmodern," one can find this model already sketched by Abraham Kuyper over a century ago (which is why Malcolm Bull once called Kuyper the "first postmodern"); this vision was extended by Herman Dooyeweerd and found a slightly different articulation in the work of Alvin Plantinga and Nicholas Wolterstorff. But I don't think this is just the property of the "Reformed" tradition. I think it is—or ought to be—a properly ecumenical and catholic vision. As such, I prefer to describe it as an "Augustinian" model.

Once we reject the monolithic construal of scholarship bequeathed to us by foundationalism and secularism, there are, I think, two ways to take up a more radical kind of Christian scholarship: one is still not radical enough, but moves in that direction.

1. The first is what I would describe as *apologetic* Christian scholarship. This mode wants to reason from explicitly Christian premises, but first attempts to earn a hearing for those commitments according to the standards of normal science in the field. In other words, apologetic Christian

scholarship (strategically, but perhaps not principally) concedes the criteria for theoretical validity to the status quo in the field and then attempts to justify Christian commitments within the rules of that game—to show that Christian claims are "rational" according to the standards of normal science. This then purchases the "right" to theorize and work from specifically Christian premises. However, the results are often minimal, and will tend to look like what I described earlier as "theistic" scholarship. But this is at least more radical than correlationist projects because it seeks to begin intentionally from "thick" Christian presuppositions.

2. The kind of scholarship that I try to advocate and practice is what we could call *unapologetic* Christian scholarship—or "unapologetics," for short. This is postfoundationalist insofar as it recognizes that what counts as "evidence" or "criteria for justification" within a given discipline is relative to a paradigm of normal science which is itself undergirded by (religious) commitments. The "rudiments of the world" (Col. 2:8) are *religious* in nature. This is "unapologetic" in the sense that (a) it does not apologize for its specifically Christian foundations and (b) it does not spend its time trying to convince the field of the justification of these commitments by the rules of normal science (because, ultimately, [i] all scholars work from *some* such commitments, and [ii] neutral agreement is not possible). Rather than apologetics, the Christian scholar engages in a kind of "unapologetics."

I think that such an unapologetic notion of Christian scholarship has several features and an important implication: unapologetics begins, unabashedly, from *revelation*—or, as Plantinga puts it, from "what we know as Christians."[26] We see the world *as* creation, or human beings *as* created in the image of God, or take a notion of sin seriously *only because* we see the world through the lens of God's revelation in Christ and Scripture. The reality of sin, for instance, is not something that is "objectively" there to be seen without seeing the world *through* the lens of God's revelation. Our acceptance of revelation is rooted in faith, and thus unapologetic Christian scholarship begins from the specificity of *Christian* faith (having recognized that all scholarship is grounded in *some* faith, so the playing field should be leveled). This is why Christian scholarship cannot be beholden to any kind of "realism" or "objectivity" in the classical sense. Instead, I would advocate what I describe as a *confessional realism*.

Unapologetics, then, refers to a vision of Christian scholarship which begins unapologetically from the "thick" presuppositions of Christian faith—precisely because we recognize that all scholarship begins from some faith. Unapologetics might also be described as "confessional theory." This stems not from a retreat from the academy into "religious" enclaves, but rather from a trenchant critique of "secular" reason which unveils that, in fact, everyone is a confessional theorist. And so why shouldn't we be able to begin from the thick particularity of a distinctly Christian vision of the world?[27]

B. After Worldview: The Christian Social Imaginary

The broader "integration" project rightly contests the lingering secularist orthodoxy within the academy.[28] That particular piece of the project I want to affirm. The problem is, as we have seen, that many particular versions of integration often continue with a sort of functional affirmation of objectivity in the disciplines, thus giving rise to a sort of syncretism or correlationism. But there is an additional problem with this model, one that attends "worldview"-talk. My concern is that worldview-talk—particularly in its recently distorted form, but also perhaps even at its best moments—still retains a picture of the human person that situates the center of gravity of human identity in the cognitive regions of the mind rather than the affective regions of the gut/heart/body. While it rejects thinking-thing-ism, it is prone to fall prey to believing-thing-ism where "beliefs" are still treated as quasi-ideas, "propositions" that require assent. In short, it still retains an emphasis on that narrow mode of cognition we might call "ratiocination," and often remains blind to the significance of the affective and bodily core of who we are. The result is a narrow, reductionistic understanding of the human person that fails to appreciate the primarily affective, non-intellectual way that we negotiate being-in-the-world.

I want to suggest that postmodern philosophical developments rightly shift the center of gravity of the human person from the cognitive to the affective, from mind to "heart." As a way of working out the implications of this for Christian scholarship, I suggest that we might consider a (temporary) moratorium on the notion of "worldview" and instead consider adopting Charles Taylor's notion of "the social imaginary."[29] Taylor is also convinced that understanding culture requires us to give up our fixation on ideas and "theory" and instead focus on the "understanding" that is embedded in practices. He emphasizes that all societies and communities are animated by a social imaginary, but this does not mean that all are oriented by a "theory." The social imaginary, he says, is "much broader and deeper than the intellectual schemes people may entertain when they *think* about social reality in a disengaged mode."[30] Taylor intuits that what we "think about"—even what we "believe"—is just the tip of the iceberg and cannot fully or even adequately account for how and why we make our way in the world. There's something else and something more rumbling beneath the cognitive that drives much of our action and behavior. Taylor describes this as an "imaginary" in order to refer to "the way ordinary people 'imagine' their social surroundings" which is "not expressed in theoretical terms, but is carried in images, stories, and legends." To call this an "imaginary" is already to shift the center of gravity from the cognitive region of ideas to the more affective region that is "closer" to the body, as it were— since the imagination runs off the fuel of the body. So "imaginary" already hints at a more embodied sense of how we are oriented in the world. The imaginary is more a kind of non-cognitive "understanding" than a cognitive "knowledge" or set of beliefs. In fact, Taylor invokes Martin Heidegger's distinction between "knowledge" (*Wissen*), which is objective and propositional, and "understanding" (*Verstehen*), which is an "inarticulate understanding of our whole situation" that constitutes the "background" of our knowledge (*Wissen*).[31] This "understanding" is more on the order of know-how than propositional knowledge, more on the order of the *imagination* than intellect. To describe this in terms of the imagination (an "imaginary") is meant to signal that our most basic way of intending and constituting the world is visceral and tactile—it runs off the fuel of "images" provided by the senses.

So when Taylor emphasizes the fundamental and necessary function of the "social *imaginary*" as a non-cognitive director of our actions and our entire comportment to the world, I think it is important to hear in that an emphasis on the imagination as an affective "faculty" that constitutes the world for us on a level that is bodily. It is a way of "intending" the world meaningfully—giving it "significance"—but in a way that is not cognitive or propositional. In common parlance we might describe it as a kind of intuition that, as Taylor observes, eludes propositional articulation: "it can never be adequately expressed in the form of explicit doctrines."[32] Instead, as something functioning on the order of the imagination rather than the intellect, a social imaginary is "often not expressed in theoretical terms, but is carried in images, stories, and legends."[33] A social imaginary is not how we *think* about the world, but how we *imagine* the world before we ever think about it; hence the social imaginary is made up of the stuff that fuels the imagination—stories, myths, pictures, narratives.[34]

This shifting of our center of gravity from the cognitive to the affective—which is the whole point of describing this as an "imaginary"—finds its completion in the role of bodily practices in this picture. Taylor emphasizes a dynamic relationship between such understanding and practice: "If the understanding makes the practice possible, it is also true that it is the practice that largely carries the understanding."[35] Or, to put it otherwise, the understanding is "implicit in practice."[36] This "understanding" is still distinct from, and irreducible to, "theoretical" or propositional knowledge. And I can—and most often *do*—function with an understanding without ever needing a "theory." Here he suggests a helpful analogy: the understanding implicit in practice is akin to knowing how to get around your neighborhood or town. This is a kind of know-how that is embedded in your adaptive unconscious. Often, if we've grown up in an area for years, we've never looked at a map of the area. Rather, we have an understanding of our environment and surroundings that has been built up from our absorption in it: we've been biking and walking these streets for years. We could get home from the ball diamond without even thinking about it. In fact, if we're a long-time resident and have never lived anywhere else, and a stranger stops us on the sidewalk and asks us how to get to Baldwin Street, we might actually be stumped because we've never really even paid attention to street signs. We know *how* to get from our house to the arena, our friend's house, and the corner store—but we "know" this in a way that doesn't translate well into giving directions to someone looking at a map. Map-knowledge of the town is very different from the sort of know-how that has been inscribed in us by years of walking home from school. Taylor is emphasizing that a social imaginary is an "understanding" of the world that functions on the same level as our home-town know-how, whereas a "theory" or "doctrine" is a kind of "knowledge" that is more akin to a map. And for most of us, most of the time, we make our way in the world without recourse to maps. And such "know-how" or understanding, Taylor emphasizes, cannot be "adequately expressed" in a map. There is a certain amount of slippage in that move. The two (understanding and knowledge) are not wholly incommensurate; what's "understood" in the practice can be somewhat articulated in theory or doctrine. However, there will always be something lost in translation. Furthermore, Taylor emphasizes the *priority of practices*. As he succinctly puts it, "Humans operated with a social imaginary well before they ever got into the business of theorizing about themselves."[37] The "social imaginary" is an affective, pre-intellectual "understanding" of the world. It is described as an "imaginary" (rather than a "theory") because it is fueled by the stuff of the imagination rather than the intellect: it is made up of, and embedded in, stories, narratives, myths, and icons. These visions capture our hearts and imaginations by "lining" our imagination, as it were—providing us with frameworks of "meaning" by which we make sense of our world and our calling in it. An irreducible understanding of the world resides in our intuitive, precognitive grasp of these stories.

Now, what does this have to do with a Christian worldview? I want to suggest that instead of thinking about "worldview" as a distinctly Christian "knowledge," we should talk about a Christian "social imaginary" that constitutes a distinctly Christian "understanding" of the world that is implicit in the practices of Christian worship. Discipleship and formation is less about erecting an edifice of Christian "knowledge" than it is a matter of developing a Christian know-how that intuitively "understands" the world in the light of the fullness of the gospel. And insofar as an understanding is implicit in practice, the practices of Christian worship are crucial—the *sine qua non*—for developing a distinctly Christian understanding of the world. The practices of Christian worship are the analogue of biking around the neighborhood, absorbing an understanding of our environment that is precognitive and becomes inscribed in our adaptive unconscious. If we map this onto Taylor's account we can see some important implications: first, if humans operate with a social imaginary well before they get into the business of cognitive "theorizing," then by analogy we could say that humans were religious well before they ever developed a theoretical theology, and for most "ordinary people" religious devotion is rarely a matter of theory.[38] Rather, there is an understanding of the world that is carried in and implicit in the practices of religious worship and devotion. These rituals form the imagination of a people who thus construe their world as a particular kind of environment based on the formation implicit in such practices. In just this sense Christianity is a unique social imaginary that "inhabits" and emerges from the matrix of preaching and prayer. The rhythms and rituals of Christian worship are not the "expression of" a Christian worldview, but are themselves an "understanding" implicit in practice—an understanding that cannot be had *apart from* the practices. It's not that we start with beliefs and doctrine and then come up with worship practices that properly "express" these (cognitive) beliefs; rather, we begin with worship and the beliefs bubble up from there. "Doctrines" are the cognitive, theoretical articulation of what we "understand" when we pray.

Second, the "understanding" implicit in practice cannot be simply identified with the sorts of ideas, beliefs, or doctrines that tend to be the currency of contemporary "worldview"-talk. The understanding—which is primary—can never be distilled into doctrines, ideas, or formulas without remainder. As Taylor emphasized, there is a kind of irreducible genius that resides in the practices—in the same way that the "understanding" that is embedded in the paintings in the Sistine Chapel are not just "substitutes" for a treatise on Pauline theology, or vice versa.[39] While aspects of the social imaginary can be articulated and expressed—and even helpfully refined and reflected upon—in cognitive, propositional terms, this can never function as a substitute for participating in the practices which themselves "carry" an understanding that eludes articulation in cognitive categories. The distillation of the Christian worldview in terms of "creation-Fall-redemption-and-consummation" can never adequately grasp what is *understood* when we participate in communion and eat the Body of Christ, broken for the renewal of a broken world. And such an understanding is the condition of possibility for any later "knowledge." Christian scholarship requires not (just) the mastery of Christian ideas and theories, nor even an understanding of a Christian "worldview," but first and fundamentally the re-shaping of the social imaginary.

III. Liturgy, Learning, and a Vision for Ecclesial Scholarship

Radical Christian scholarship will be scholarship that begins unapologetically from a Christian "understanding" of the world.[40] This means that one of the crucial issues for the project of Christian scholarship is discerning *how* this "understanding" is formed. Once again, I think our philosophical anthropology is important here. While scholars are the sorts of strange creatures who spend a good deal of their day engaged in cognitive, theoretical modes of engaging the world, this does not mean that scholars are "thinking things" as if they were some sort of exception to the affective anthropology I've sketched above. Scholars are fundamentally *affective* animals, too.[41] That means the theoretical work of scholarship is oriented by pre-theoretical understanding, by the shape of our social imaginary. So integral Christian scholarship needs to be nourished by a Christian social imaginary. How is a Christian social imaginary formed? I want to suggest two primary, related modes of formation: through indwelling of the narrative of Scripture and through the formative practices of Christian worship.

A. The Conversion of the Imagination: Re-Narrating Christian Scholarship

If radical, unapologetic Christian scholarship begins from "what we know as Christians"—from the particularity of the "understanding" embedded in Christian worship—then we need to think further about the relationship between Christian scholarship and the Bible. Here I think we have serious work to do, and Christian scholars seem reticent to visit the issue because it feels like a certain lapse into biblicism. For many of us, we became engaged in the cultural work of scholarship precisely because we had overcome the dualisms of "Bible-only" accounts that disparaged "the world." And so I recognize that a call to Christian scholars to take the Bible seriously can be an occasion for folks to get a tad nervous.

But consider the project: If we are working with an understanding of Christian scholarship that makes *revelation* central, then mustn't we grapple with Scripture as a primary site of God's revelation? And yet, it is somewhat embarrassing to note the degree of biblical illiteracy among "Christian scholars" and the lack of sophistication we have when dealing with biblical text (if we ever do!). To pick on my own discipline, Christian philosophers often indicate the importance of revelation for Christian theorizing, and sometimes refer to Scripture, but too often it is in the mode of "proof-texting," drawing on a less-than-sufficient acquaintance with the Bible that tends to de-contextualize Scripture, wresting passages from their canonical and historical context and reducing them to propositions for logical operations. I've come to feel that this is deeply insufficient.[42]

I don't mean to suggest that every Christian scholar should also be a biblical scholar (though I would consider it a happy coincidence were we to find a few folks who embodied both of these gifts!). Nor do I mean to grant a license to Christian scholars from every discipline to freelance as amateur biblical scholars. Rather, I'm suggesting that if revelation is to be central to Christian theorizing, then we ought to draw on that well of revelation with the best possible pail. When our philosophical investigations bring us into conversation with, say, the social sciences, we try to draw on the best scholarship in the field; the same should be the case when we engage the Scriptures (particularly in my model of confessional theory, where Christian scholarship must draw on revelation).

To that end, I think there is a dire need for professional development opportunities that provide venues for Christian scholars to become acquainted with the best work in biblical studies and biblical theology (a field that is undergoing upheaval in some very interesting, confessional directions).[43] And I think a more robust engagement with Scripture could also open up interesting, productive research agendas. We have seen this happen when the disciplines have engaged theology (e.g., philosophers picking up on Calvin's notion of the *sensus divinitatis* gave birth to "Reformed epistemology," and in psychology we are beginning to see models that explicitly engage Trinitarian theology); in the same way, engagement with biblical studies (and more specifically, the *theological* interpretation of Scripture) could provide a fund for theory that we could not imagine otherwise.[44]

Let me put the point this way: the vision of "unapologetic" Christian scholarship that I have sketched appreciates that all scholarship (even scholarship which pretends to be "secular") is nourished and governed by a "worldview"—a constellation of beliefs and commitments that shape how one sees the world. Appreciating this nonfoundationalist situation (a leveling of the playing field, we might say), unapologetics then envisions a kind of Christian scholarship that draws on the thickness and specificity of a distinctly Christian worldview.[45] Now, if a "thick" Christian worldview is to inform scholarship (if we are going to begin from "what we know as Christians" [Plantinga]), then we need to engage the riches of Scripture and the unfolding of the biblical narrative. Our engagements with Scripture—like all modes of reading—is always already *interpretation* under the conditions of "background" and horizons of expectation.[46] We always approach Scripture with an *interpretive stance* (Bockmuehl). So the question is: which interpretive stance is appropriate for understanding Scripture in a way that can inform Christian scholarship? While I don't have space to unpack this in detail here, I would argue that we ought to engage Scripture *canonically* and/ or *theologically*—taking the Bible as the church's book, the script of a worshiping community.[47] The insights Scripture will yield will not be discrete "gems" (read: prooftexts) to be mined from the raw material of the text; rather they will be tropes disclosed in the context of the narrative—which requires that we are not only familiar with the plot, but immersed in the plot, seeing ourselves in the story. So I think that it is important for Christian scholars to engage Scripture with at least two interests in mind:

(1) Insofar as Christian scholarship entails the articulation of *theory*, then the "thickness" of the biblical understanding of the world should inform the Christian worldview that informs theory formation. Theory formation always involves some element of *normativity*, and those norms come from pre-theoretical sources (viz., worldviews).[48] So, for instance, theories in psychology and sociology will assume some normative picture of what human persons are and what constitutes human flourishing. Those norms are not yielded "scientifically"; rather, they are pre-scientific and are the norms that *orient* science. A distinctly Christian psychology or sociology would articulate norms of human flourishing that are primarily informed by Christian revelation (even though one might also then try to "translate" them into a more general form for broader academic dialogue). For projects of theory formation, Scriptural engagement can be a source of *content*, pointing us to resources that "fill in" the Christian worldview (or theology.

(2) However, there is also a second, and broader, way in which Scriptural engagement is important for Christian scholarship. To be a Christian scholar is to see and understand the world through the lens of the Christian social imaginary. As such, this requires forming *habits of seeing*, habits of being attuned and attentive to the world in a way that reflects Christian concern. How does that happen? Well, one of the primary ways this happens is through "eating the Word" (Eugene Peterson). Or, as Richard Hays puts it, learning to read Scripture well is a means for the "conversion of the imagination."[49] He is particularly interested in encouraging contemporary readers to follow the example of Paul's reading of Israel's Scripture: "if we do follow his example, the church's imagination will be converted to see both Scripture and the world in a radically new way."[50] This "conversion of the imagination" by reading Scripture happens primarily, I would contend, when Scripture is encountered *liturgically* (communally in worship). However, it can also happen through

intentional *study*. So even if Scripture never makes a showing in the specific content of our scholarship, we should nevertheless be a people—and a community of scholars—whose imaginations are habituated to seeing the world through the imaginative plot and categories of Scripture.

This points to a second and final implication of "unapologetics" that I would like to note—an implication that points to a crucial overlap between our tasks as scholars and our tasks as teachers.

B. *The Liturgical Imagination: (Re)Forming Christian Scholars*

My vision of unapologetics or confessional theory has a second trajectory of implication. If our thinking at its root is to be governed and shaped by the "thick" elements of Christian confession, then we need to consider just how we can be equipped for this task. In order to *practice* such an unapologetics, we need to be *formed by* this revelation and learn to see the world *through* that lens. In Hays' terms, our imaginations must undergo conversion—again and again! To have our imagination shaped by the narrative of Scripture is to be narrated *by* the story, to absorb this revelation into our identity. And the primary site for the absorption of revelation is the worship of the church (contrary to individualistic pictures of the lone Christian in her closet with her Bible, mining it for propositions). It is worship (in the full-orbed sense of Word and sacrament) which transforms or renews the mind—granting us what Linda Zagzebski describes as "virtues of the mind." In this way, the foolish darkening of our hearts (Rom. 1:21ff.) is undone and we begin to see the world *as* creation.

Therefore, I would argue that worship, liturgy, and the church are absolutely central to radical Christian scholarship—and to the Christian scholar. Our work as Christian scholars needs to be oriented by an imagination that is infused with the story of God's work in the world. Participation in the liturgical life of the church is necessary for the sanctification that makes Christian scholarship possible, because it is in the affectivity of the liturgy that our imagination is fueled and shaped by the gospel.[51] As Augustine emphasized in *On True Religion*, the mind needs healing in order to see well.

At this point, some Christian scholars get a bit skittish; they worry that such a proposal sounds like a retreat back to pietism where "Christian scholars" are just scholars who go to church, or that what makes a college Christian is the chapel. But what I'm advocating is a post-critical, post-pietistic recovery of the central role of worship and the church for the task of Christian scholarship. "Pietism" fails to advocate unapologetics precisely because it fails to discern an integral, theoretical connection between the chapel and the classroom. In the pietistic (correlationist) model, the chapel sanctifies the classroom and laboratory *by addition*. It (unwittingly) concedes the space of the classroom and the laboratory to the standards of "normal science." But we have roundly criticized such correlationist models.

Ironically, those Christian scholars who resist my suggested centrality of worship and church for the task of Christian scholarship tend to reflect an over-correction which mirrors a similar distorted picture of the task of Christian scholarship. If pietistic correlationism thinks it's the chapel that makes the college Christian, in a strange way, those opposed to pietism almost seem to think the chapel *compromises* the task of "integral" Christian scholarship. ("Students would be better off spending time hunkered down in the library!," I've heard colleagues say.) But this actually perpetuates the dualism of the pietistic or correlationist model: it doesn't think worship, liturgy, or the church really touches the work of Christian scholarship and Christian learning. Both of these models assume a dualistic philosophical anthropology which sees the mind or intellect as the "site" for Christian scholarship and Christian learning, and sees worship and liturgy as dealing with the affections (the "heart"). But the unapologetics I am sketching refuses such dualisms. In league with Augustine and Jonathan Edwards, it emphasizes that we are primarily *affective* animals—that the work of the intellect is embedded in the ether of the imagination, which is itself intimately tethered to the body and thus bodily rhythms and rituals. Christian scholarship and Christian teaching, then, are not *primarily* about *ideas*; they are concerned with the formation of the *imagination*, and that happens largely (but not only) through affective means. In particular, it happens through the affective media of symbol, sign, and story—just the sort of world one finds in the practices of liturgy and worship.

On this point, let me register one further protest against formulas for "integrating" faith and learning, *viz.*, the generic character of "faith" in these discussions.[52] To put this otherwise, I have concerns about what we mean by a *Christian* college. What is "Christianity" without the church? What if instead of shaping *Christian* colleges and *Christian* scholarship, we think about *ecclesial* colleges and *ecclesial* scholarship?[53] I want to argue that this "faith" needs to be specified, and such specification happens not primarily in the articulation of propositions or the distillation of Christian "ideas," but in the liturgy and worship life of the church. Thus, instead of retaining the notion of "worldview" (which feels a bit heady and cognitive), we might appropriate Charles Taylor's notion of a "social imaginary"—which emphasizes both the central role of imagination, as well as the embedding of a social imaginary in practices. Before a social imaginary is articulated as ideas, it is *lived* as a constellation of practices. This means that the task of Christian scholarship requires the formation of the imagination, which requires that we be immersed in the practices which form our "imaginary." That happens primarily in the embodied, affective, communal liturgical practices of the church— some of which are also staged on a daily basis within our academic communities. Thus unapologetics, while rejecting the correlationist and pietist notion that the chapel "sanctifies" the classroom and laboratory, actually recovers a more integral and fundamental role for worship and liturgy as the condition of possibility for Christian scholarship.

Chapter 1 Notes

1. Since this chapter began its life as a talk at Indiana Wesleyan University, a number of elements of the argument have been refined and expanded in James K. A. Smith, *Desiring the Kingdom: Worship, Worldview, and Cultural Formation* (Grand Rapids, MI: Baker Academic, 2009).

2. Cf. Calvin Seerveld, "A Tin Can Theory of the Human Person," in *In the Fields of the Lord: A Calvin Seerveld Reader*, ed. Craig Bartholomew (Toronto: Tuppence, 2000).

3. Francis Beckwith, "Introduction," in *To Everyone an Answer: A Case for the Christian Worldview*, eds. Francis Beckwith, William Lane Craig, and J. P. Moreland (Downers Grove, IL: InterVarsity Press, 2004), 14.

4. Kenneth Richard Samples, *A World of Difference: Putting Christian Truth-Claims to the Worldview Test* (Grand Rapids, MI: Baker, 2007), 15. For other popular accounts along these rationalist lines, see The Truth Project from Focus on the Family or Brannon Howse's "Worldview Weekend." I would also point out the ineluctable politics of such worldview talk. For Beckwith, Samples, Charles Colson, and others, the adoption of "worldview-talk" has been linked to a political project of "transforming" America (or "taking America back for God"). This is seen starkly in Samples' opening vignette that highlights the "worldview" difference between "American President George W. Bush [a 'devout evangelical Christian'] and Muslim extremist Osama bin Laden" (Samples, 12-13). In other words, the rationalist hijacking of worldview talk is coincident with the enlistment of worldview talk in the culture wars. Cf. also J. P. Moreland and William Lane Craig, *Philosophical Foundations for a Christian Worldview* (Downers Grove, IL: InterVarsity Press, 2003), who emphasize the importance of understanding "the Christian worldview" precisely in order to secure its cultural dominance: "The average Christian does not realize that there is an intellectual struggle going on in the universities. . . . Enlightenment naturalism and postmodern anti-realism are arrayed in an unholy alliance against a broadly theistic and specifically Christian worldview." [Up for a Crusade, anyone?] Thus they admonish: "Christians cannot afford to be indifferent to the outcome of this struggle. . . . If the Christian worldview can be restored to a place of prominence and respect at the university, it will have a leavening effect throughout society. If we change the university, we change our culture through those who shape culture" (1-2). Christian philosophers are now arrayed "like Gideon's army" on this battlefront (3-4). (It might also be noted that their book was funded in part by the Discovery Institute [8].)

5. Abraham Kuyper famously articulated Calvinism as a "world- and life-view" in his 1898 Stone Lectures at Princeton University. See Kuyper, *Calvinism* (Grand Rapids, MI: Eerdmans, 1943).

6. For articulations within this tradition, see Albert Wolters, *Creation Regained*; James H. Olthuis, "On Worldviews," in *Stained Glass*; Brian J. Walsh and J. Richard Middleton, *The Transforming Vision*; Cornelius Plantinga, *Engaging God's World*. For my affirmation of this richer understanding of worldview, and a clarification of my critique, see James K. A. Smith, "Worldview, Sphere Sovereignty, and *Desiring the Kingdom*: A Guide for (Perplexed) Reformed Folk," *Pro Rege* 39.4 (June 2011): 15-24.

7. However, I would note that even those Reformational articulations of worldview that have sensed a problem with the "thinking thing" cognitivism of the tradition have still tended to let "knowledge" retain the center of gravity—thus talking about

"knowing" other-wise.See, e.g., John Kok, ed., *Ways of Knowing: In Concert* (Sioux Center, IA: Dordt Press, 2005) and James H. Olthuis, ed., *Knowing* Other-*wise: Philosophy at the Threshold of Spirituality* (Bronx, NY: Fordham University Press, 1997). The centrality and privilege of *knowledge* is a hard habit to break. Below I will engage Martin Heidegger's and Charles Taylor's notion of "understanding" (*Verstehen*) as a way to de-center this privilege on knowing. However, even this clearly has limits since "understanding" is still within the semantic range of things we associate with knowing (i.e., "understanding" still sounds like the sort of thing that "thinking things" do). Perhaps when I articulate this in terms of *imagination* we'll be on to a real alternative.

8. For an expansion on this point, see Smith, *Desiring the Kingdom*, chapters 4-5.

9. Cf. Samples' and Barna's specific claims on this point. Critiquing this sort of picture (whether liberal or conservative), Stanley Hauerwas comments: "Such a strategy assumes that what makes a Christian is holding certain beliefs that help us better understand the human condition, to make sense of our experience. Of course no one denies that those beliefs may have behavioral implications, but the assumption is that the beliefs must be in place in order for the behavior to be authentic" (Hauerwas, *After Christendom? How the Church Is to Behave if Freedom, Justice, and a Christian Nation Are Bad Ideas* [Nashville: Abingdon, 1999], 95). In addition to working with a flawed anthropology that prioritizes "cerebral" belief over embodied action, Hauerwas also notes the individualism of such a picture: "When Christianity is understood fundamentally as a belief system necessary for people to give meaning to their lives, we cannot but continue to reinforce the assumption that salvation is for the individual. It is one of the ironies of our time that many of those who are identified with urging Christians to engage in politics in the name of their Christian beliefs hold what are fundamentally individualistic [and cognitivist, I would add] accounts of Christian salvation. They assume that Christianity entails social engagement, but salvation was still identified with the individual coming to a better self-understanding through the world view offered by Christianity" (96). It is a further irony that folk like Samples, Colson, et. al., who adopt such a "worldview" orientation to underwrite the politics of culture war are, in fact, mimicking an essentially *liberal* strategy that Hauerwas critiques in Niebuhr [180n.5].

10. See James K. A. Smith, *Introducing Radical Orthodoxy: Mapping a Post-Secular Theology* (Grand Rapids, MI: Baker Academic, 2004), ch. 5.

11. For a critique of such projects for a "universal" or "generic" ethics or "morality," see John Milbank, "Can Morality be Christian?," in *The Word Made Strange* (Oxford: Blackwell, 1997) and Stanley Hauerwas, *The Peaceable Kingdom: A Primer in Christian Ethics* (Notre Dame, IN: University of Notre Dame Press, 1983), where he emphasizes that there is no "generic" ethic; every ethic is qualified by a narrative and a tradition. For discussion of these points, see Smith, *Introducing Radical Orthodoxy*, 240-243.

12. I take exception to Alvin Plantinga's equation of the two when he speaks of "Christianity or Christian theism" (as in his Stob Lectures, "The Twin Pillars of Christian Scholarship," in *Seeking Understanding: The Stob Lectures, 1986-1998* [Grand Rapids, MI: Eerdmans, 2001], 125; or "Advice to Christian Philosophers") and then in a slightly different version at Notre Dame speaks of "Christianity or Christian theism, or Judeo-Christian theism." I prefer when he speaks of "positive Christian science" (*The Stob Lectures*, 139).

13. For further discussion of "correlationist" approaches, see Smith, *Introducing Radical Orthodoxy*, 35-37 and 148-153.

14. As just one example of this sort of claim to "presuppositionlessness," I recently ran into Freud's "History of the Psychoanalytic Movement" in which he emphasizes that he didn't read Nietzsche "with the conscious motive of not wishing to be hindered in the work out of my psychoanalytic impressions by any preconceived ideas" (in *The Basic Writings of Sigmund Freud*, ed. A. A. Brill [New York: The Modern Library, 1938], 939). He later claims that he "was subject to no influences" (943).

15. See Kant, "What Is Enlightenment?"

16. Akin to Rawls' "original position."

17. See especially James K. A. Smith, *Who's Afraid of Postmodernism? Taking Derrida, Lyotard, and Foucault to Church* (Grand Rapids, MI: Baker Academic, 2006).

18. Thus Bruce Ellis Benson compares the postmodern critique with prophetic critique in *Graven Ideologies: Nietzsche, Derrida, and Marion on Idolatry* (Downers Grove, IL: InterVarsity Press, 2002).

19. I have developed this in much more detail in James K. A. Smith, *The Fall of Interpretation: Philosophical Foundations for a Creational Hermeneutic*, 2nd ed. (Grand Rapids, MI: Baker Academic, 2012).

20. For more on tradition, see ibid., ch. 5.

21. See also Bruce Ellis Benson, "Paul and the Knowledge that Puffs Up: A Taste for Idolatry," *Journal of Philosophy and Scripture* 2.2 (Spring 2005), http://philosophyandscripture.org/Issue2-2/Benson/benson.html.

22. The theme of being "rooted" is important in the context of Colossians. See, for example, Colossians 2:7. This organic metaphor in Colossians is usually coupled with an architectural metaphor of "foundations" on which we are "established" and "built up."

23. For a discussion of the point, see George Marsden, *The Outrageous Idea of Christian Scholarship* (New York: Oxford University Press, 1997).

24. For a non-Christian critique of secularism and *apologia* for genuine pluralism (a pluralism which also makes room for faith commitments), see William Connolly, *Why I Am Not a Secularist* (Minneapolis: University of Minnesota Press, 2000), and more recently, William Connolly, *Pluralism* (Durham, NC: Duke University Press, 2005).

25. This will also require that we give up any "Constantinian" vision of Christian scholarship as somehow part of a project to "take over" the academy and "bring it to [Christian] Reason." I fear that the expanding interest of evangelical scholars in "natural law" is an indicator of just such hegemonic, anti-pluralist projects. I hope to unpack this concern in more detail elsewhere.

26. See Plantinga, *Stob Lectures*, 135, 143, 144, 160. He also speaks of "the deliverances of faith" (159).

27. Cf. Marsden, *Outrageous Idea of Christian Scholarship*, Afterword. For further discussion of this point, see Smith, *Introducing Radical Orthodoxy*, 73-74 and ch. 5.

28. This is nicely outlined and summarized in Todd C. Ream and Perry L. Glanzer, *Christian Faith and Scholarship: An Exploration of Contemporary Developments*, ASHE Higher Education Report 33.2 (San Francisco: Jossey-Bass, 2007).

29. Charles Taylor, *Modern Social Imaginaries* (Durham, NC: Duke University Press, 2004), 23-30, now expanded in Taylor, *A Secular Age*, 171-176. For this concept, Taylor acknowledges his debt to Benedict Anderson, *Imagined Communities* (London: Verso, 1991).

30. Taylor, *Modern Social Imaginaries*, 23, emphasis added.

31. Ibid., 25, drawing particularly on Hubert Dreyfus's reading of Heidegger in *Being-in-the-World* (Cambridge, MA: MIT Press, 1991). For the relevant discussion in

Heidegger, see *Being and Time*, §31. Heidegger's articulation grows out of a critique of Husserl's "cognitivism"—a charge echoed by Dreyfus. For a defense of Husserl in this regard, see Christian Lotz, "Cognitivism and Practical Intentionality: A Critique of Dreyfus's Critique of Husserl," *International Philosophical Quarterly* 47 (2007): 153-166. Taylor finds analogous notions of "understanding" in Wittgenstein and Polanyi.

32. Taylor, *Modern Social Imaginaries*, 25.

33. Ibid., 23.

34. Here there is an important resonance between Taylor's account and Christian Smith's claim that human beings are "narrative" animals. "For all our science, rationality, and technology," Smith observes, "we moderns are no less the makers, tellers, and believers of narrative construals of existence, history, and purpose than were our forebears at any other time in human history. But more than that, we not only continue to be animals who makes stories but also animals who are *made by* our stories" (*Moral, Believing Animals*, 64). Thus Smith is also contesting cognitivist accounts of the human person. This gets tethered to embodied practice in his discussion of "liturgies" that make up moral orders (16).

35. Taylor, *Modern Social Imaginaries*, 25.

36. Ibid., 26. We might quibble with Taylor here a bit. While he wants to emphasize that the relationship between "imaginary" (understanding) and practice is "not one-sided" (25), there does seem to be some ambiguity in his account. At times he speaks as if the understanding "makes possible" common practices (23), as if practices "express" a pre-existent understanding. However, at other times Taylor emphasizes that it is the practices that "carry" the understanding (25). While I think he is right to honor the dynamic, dialectical relation between the two, I think it particularly important to emphasize the latter. If there is a priority in this chicken-or-the-egg-like question, I would think the practices precede the understanding. As he later emphasizes, "Ideas [and so, *mutatis mutandis*, understanding] always come in history wrapped up in certain practices" (33).

37. Ibid., 26.

38. Taylor's model can account for a dynamic that needs to be recognized here, *viz.*, that "theory" sometimes "trickles down" and "infiltrates" the social imaginary (24). In fact, he thinks this is exactly what happened in modernity: the "ideas" of Grotius and Locke gradually "infiltrate and transform" our social imaginary, producing what will become the unique understanding embedded in the *modern* social imaginary (28-29). [Heidegger has a similar account of how theory can become "sedimented" into our understanding, BT, §62.] I would suggest something similar happens in the case of Christian worship: the "fruit" of theological reflection (e.g., the Nicene Creed) trickles down and infiltrates the Christian social imaginary such that this now becomes absorbed as a kind of non-cognitive "understanding." I suggested something like this in *Introducing Radical Orthodoxy*, 178-179.

39. This analogy is suggested in Gordon Graham's discussion of the irreducibility of artistic "truth" in Gordon Graham, *Philosophy of the Arts*, 2nd ed. (Routledge, 2000), 46-51. Art's "understanding" should not be reduced to the sense of "assent to propositions," in which case art would be only one medium of many alternatives which can communicate propositional truth. Graham emphasizes that art cannot be "paraphrased" (51), nor can it be simply "exchanged" with other media for the same purpose. In the same way, theories and practices are not simply convertible; one can't drop the practice once one "gets" the theory.

40. This assumes the "postmodern" critique which levels the playing field by pointing out that *all* scholars begin with *some* (pre-scientific, pre-rational, faith-like) "understanding" of the world.

41. Christian Smith makes the same point when he emphasizes that social scientists are not exempt from being narrative animals: "Sociologists not only make stories but are animals who are made by their stories. . . . No one, not even the statistics-laden sociologist, escapes the moral, believing, narrative-constituted condition of the human animal" (*Moral, Believing Animals* [New York: Oxford University Press, 2003], 87). In the same vein, "all human persons, no matter how well educated, how scientific, how knowledgeable, are, at bottom, *believers*" (54).

42. I think this situation ultimately indicates the failure of our churches to form us by the narrative of Scripture.

43. For an excellent primer on the theological interpretation of Scripture, see J. Todd Billings, *The Word of God for the People of God: An Entryway to the Theological Interpretation of Scripture* (Grand Rapids, MI: Eerdmans, 2010).

44. Cf. Walter Brueggemann's suggestion regarding the productive possibilities of engaging Scripture to think about the task of education in Walter Brueggemann, *The Creative Word: Canon as a Model for Biblical Education* (Philadelphia: Fortress Press, 1982), 2-3.

45. Because I want Christian scholarship to draw on the "thick" resources of the Christian faith, I am somewhat hesitant just to describe this as a "worldview," since worldview-talk tends to settle for a very thin, diluted account of the faith (e.g., creation-fall-redemption) and fails to draw on the specificity of the riches of the Christian story. Thus, in *Introducing Radical Orthodoxy* I talk about Christian scholarship being oriented and governed by "theology," or more specifically, what I call theology$_1$. See *Introducing Radical Orthodoxy*, 166-179.

46. See Smith, *The Fall of Interpretation*, ch. 6.

47. Again, see Billings, *Word of God for the People of God*, for an argument about the ecclesial and liturgical "home" of Scripture.

48. Cf. Christian Smith, *Moral, Believing Animals*.

49. Richard B. Hays, *The Conversion of the Imagination: Paul as Interpreter of Israel's Scripture* (Grand Rapids, MI: Eerdmans, 2005), viii.

50. Ibid. He goes on to point out that this is as old as Origen: "As a Christian interpreter living in a pagan world, Origen was able to see clearly that Gentile converts to the faith needed to have their minds re-made, and that instruction in how to read Scripture was at the heart of Paul's pastoral practice: Gentiles needed to be initiated into reading practices that enabled them to receive Israel's Scripture as their own."

51. Not just some "principles" of creation or justice, but the thick specificities of God in Christ reconciling the world to himself.

52. I have voiced a similar concern about the generic character of evangelical Christian faith in my "Between the University and the Church: The Precarious (and Promising) Site of Campus Ministry," *Anastasis* 1.2 (2002): 3-4.

53. Cf. Wright and Budde, *Conflicting Allegiances: The Church-Based University in a Liberal Democratic Society* (Grand Rapids, MI: Brazos, 2004).

HEALING DEMOCRACY'S DISCONTENT

The Christian Contribution to Contemporary Politics

Jeanne Heffernan Schindler

My interest in the study of the relationship shared by political science and the Christian faith is inspired by the rather curious position of the Christian scholar who by his very nature is committed not only to a set of disciplinary propositions but to a personal God who famously, even surprisingly, said of himself: "I am the Truth." Thus, the discipleship of a Christian scholar—and student, for that matter—entails a devotion to the Truth simply; we cannot maintain a division between faith and learning when the God in whom we place our faith is the same God who created the matter for every conceivable area of inquiry.

Right from the outset, then, we can affirm that a Christian approach to learning is inextricably, from first to last, informed by faith. And according to Christian faith, God reveals his wisdom and love through the Book of Revelation *and* the Book of Nature; faith *and* human reason both yield truths that originate with the Author of Truth. As Ambrose of Milan affirmed, "Anything true, by no matter whom it is said, is from the Holy Spirit."[1]

The unity of truth lends dignity to the investigation of the whole of reality, sacred and mundane, as each bears the stamp of God's creative love. In the words of John Henry Newman, "All that is good, all that is true, all that is beautiful, all that is beneficent, be it great or small, be it perfect or fragmentary, natural as well as supernatural, moral as well as material, comes from Him."[2] Like a great mosaic whose individual tiles are indispensable to the integrity of the whole image, the structure of the university should reflect, indeed radiate, this unity of truth; but it is precisely this unity that has been eroding since the nineteenth century. Sensitive observers like Newman perceived this keenly. He observed a mortal threat to the integrity of the university from the twin impulses of utilitarianism and secularism, each of which would imperil the place of theology in what we would today call the "core curriculum." In *The Idea of a University*, Newman argued persuasively that an education must include theological study, since the discipline of theology has the unique capacity to answer foundational questions *presupposed* by the other fields of inquiry. Without theology's irreplaceable competence, Newman insisted, every discipline would suffer. This holds true for political science, my area of study, no less than the fields explicitly identified by Newman. Likewise, I would argue, theology needs political science. Without it, theology would find itself bereft of important insights about how a community lives together well. There is an indispensable, though asymmetrical, reciprocity here.

This might seem a strange contention, especially today, an age suspicious of any intermingling of religion and politics. But I think that Newman is right. If the structure and curriculum of the university is not faithful to the unity of truth, education is lost, and if politics is studied, as it is in many, many colleges, as a field susceptible only to descriptive, putatively "scientific" analysis, it will never be understood. It will be rendered trivial, a banal and boring collection of data shorn of any connection to those things that truly animate us: love, beauty, wisdom, truth. One has only to cast a glance at the paper titles of the annual American Political Science Association meeting for conclusive evidence: a hundred regression analyses of state legislatures. Economics is not the only dismal science.

The proper remedy for this problem, it seems to me, is to recover the classical and Christian meaning of political philosophy. This would entail a radical refusal to accept the reductive account of politics found in modern political science, whose account of politics can be thought of in terms of an etymological error: *politics*, for the moderns, might just as well have been a word stemming from *poly* (many) and *ticks* (blood-sucking parasites). As Machiavelli candidly acknowledges, "[I]t is so far from how one lives to how one should live that he who lets go of what is done for what should be done learns his ruin rather than his preservation. For a man who wants to make a profession of good in all regards must come to ruin among so many who are not good." Politics is a dangerous arena of power struggles and rival self-interests. "Hence," the clever Florentine continues, "it is necessary to a prince, if he wants to maintain himself, to learn to be able not to be good, and to use this and not use it according to necessity."[3] This renders politics a most depressing enterprise; it has lost its polestars of happiness and virtue, a fact made explicit by the other great founder of modern political thought, Thomas Hobbes. In a bold rejection of the first premise of ancient political philosophy, Hobbes asserts, "[T]he Felicity of this life, consisteth not in the repose of a mind satisfied. For there is no such Finis ultimus, (utmost ayme,) nor Summum Bonum, (greatest Good) as is spoken of in the Books of the old Morall Philosphers."[4] No longer able to identify man's highest end, we can nevertheless identify his worst evil—a violent death—and construct a political order to remedy it. If it can't save our soul, at least it can save our skin.

Just as Machiavelli and Hobbes attempted to bracket the practice of politics from the influence (and constraints) of higher fields, like theology, philosophy, and ethics, so too has modern political science attempted to bracket the study of politics from the influence of the very same fields. Eager to mimic the methods of the natural sciences, it has adopted what E. F. Schumacher aptly describes as a "methodical aversion to the recognition of higher levels . . . of significance."[5] This approach, of its very nature, is ill-equipped to resolve our most pressing political and social questions. But all is not lost.

Happily, the classical and Christian understanding of politics is still available to us, and it remedies the sterility caused by the disciplinary boundaries we have inherited. According to the ancients and the Christians alike, political philosophy was the love of wisdom concerning the things of the *polis*. For such luminaries as Plato and Aristotle, the search for wisdom about the city—that is, how we can live together well—entailed a comprehensive inquiry into the nature of man. No stripped-down, descriptive account would do, since even seemingly simple political questions, like levying a particular tax, implicated the cardinal virtue of justice, which itself was embedded in an entire anthropology. "To render each man his due," in its classical formulation, presupposed an understanding of what a man is. A "scientific" analysis of politics alone would not yield this insight; rather, many philosophical avenues of inquiry are required—metaphysics, ethics, and epistemology, to name a few.

Ancient political thought was precisely this kind of multifaceted enterprise, one that yielded rich fruit, both for philosophy and political science. Plato and Aristotle discovered that man is qualitatively different from every other living being, that he is possessed of an extraordinary power—reason—which, if used well, enables him to navigate the world and strive for happiness through the cultivation of virtue. And they perceived that politics, in its authentic sense, is a high enterprise whose object is to foster the flourishing of citizens precisely by cultivating their virtue.

The Christian contribution to political philosophy raises the stakes yet further, as it offers crucial insights about the human person that were not available to the ancients. Scripture and the Christian tradition affirm a transcendent origin and destiny of man. We are both created by God and vested by him with a supernatural end: communion with God and the saints in a state of perfect happiness. As John Paul II expressed it in his 1995 encyclical *Evangelium Vitae* (*The Gospel of Life*), "Man is called to a fullness of life which far exceeds the dimensions of his earthly existence, because it consists in sharing the very life of God. The loftiness of this supernatural vocation reveals the greatness and the inestimable value of human life even in its temporal phase." Though heaven is our final end and life on earth is only a "penultimate" reality, it is nevertheless "a sacred reality entrusted to us, to be preserved with a sense of responsibility and brought to perfection in love and in the gift of ourselves to God and to our brothers and sisters."[6]

This kind of knowledge is the fruit of revelation. God has graciously revealed that we were created out of love, for love, and in the image of a God who has suffered on our behalf so as to be reunited with us eternally. These facts shed a whole new light on the nature of man, and a Christian anthropology, in turn, illuminates the meaning of politics. For one, it supplies a crucial foundation for justice, *the* social virtue, namely, that every individual—irrespective of age, capacities, or social standing—possesses an inviolable dignity and a transcendent destiny. Under the Christian dispensation, what is man's due (as the ancients would put it)? Love, a love that enables him to flourish now and forever.

The political promise of a Christian vision of man becomes clearer when we explore our cultural context. Recall that I began this chapter by affirming the interdependence of faith and learning and by cautioning against an artificial and finally untenable division of knowledge; then I attempted to make this concrete by showing the ways in which a field of inquiry like political science presupposes knowledge which it cannot of itself attain; it is dependent upon other fields, such as philosophy and theology, for its own proper functioning. Regrettably, the contemporary state of the university on this score is dire. As Wendell Berry keenly observes in his provocative piece, aptly entitled "The Loss of the University," higher education in this country has become incoherent, its unity sacrificed to all manner of specialization. Skeptical that it can offer a unified and substantive vision of education, its default mode is to provide "training" and "skills" in a thousand sub-specialties so as to equip students for the transient requirements of the working world rather than to offer them wisdom for meeting life's most important, perennial experiences: birth, death, love, suffering, friendship, a longing for transcendence. H. J. Massingham, to whom Berry appeals, summarizes the problem in this way. "Modern knowledge," he laments, "is departmentalized." But, he insists, "the essence of culture is initiation into wholeness, so that all the divisions of knowledge are considered as the branches of one tree, the Tree of Life whose roots go deep into the earth and whose top is in heaven." [7] This is a beautifully organic vision of learning.

Alas, it has been very nearly lost. We have, instead, hyper-specialized fields without a common bond to secure their larger meaning, and this problem is not confined to the academy. Indeed, we find an analogous situation in American politics, which, like the university, has suffered a similarly fateful division. As I hope to explain, our prevailing political theory denies to our political practice the philosophical and theological resources it needs to thrive. It requires, quite illegitimately, I will argue, that we bracket our most important moral and religious commitments when entering the public square.

This problem has been well perceived by Michael Sandel. In his persuasive analysis, the problem—what he terms "democracy's discontent"—is essentially two-fold: "One is the fear that, individually and collectively, we are losing control of the forces that govern our lives. The other is the sense that, from family to neighborhood to nation, the moral fabric of community is unraveling around us."[8] He further observes that behind these concerns and complicating them, in fact, is deep disagreement over such basic notions as the nature of freedom and the purpose of politics.

For Sandel, the way in which a given political theory understands freedom and politics is critical to its potential for addressing the ailments of our polity. Rival political theories that have competed for primacy as America's public philosophy have invested the concept of freedom with vastly different meaning and so have envisioned the role of government in the lives of its citizens in vastly different terms. Now Sandel considers procedural liberalism *the* dominant public philosophy of our day. Yet, while it enjoys this status and has for the past century, he argues that its adequacy is doubtful. It cannot remedy the ills that afflict us; specifically, liberalism cannot on its own terms repair the loss of our self-government or the erosion of our communities. Why not? In Sandel's reckoning, liberalism's deficiency stems from an impoverished anthropology and political vision.

It works with a "voluntarist"[9] conception of the self, the self as an individual agent independent of and prior to his ends. It places primacy upon the individual as a bearer of rights and seeks to protect these rights against the encroachments of other individuals or of the state. Freedom is construed as the ability to select one's life goals using the means of one's choosing so long as those means are not deemed harmful to another—and what is considered harmful is understood in ever narrower, material terms. Relatedly, government in the procedural liberal scheme ostensibly adopts a stance of neutrality with respect to the life plans of its citizens and largely forsakes its educative, character-building function in favor of a regulatory one. Appealing to Rawls, Sandel summarizes the point this way: "The liberal state . . . does not discriminate;

none of its policies or laws may presuppose that any person or way of life is intrinsically more virtuous than any other. It respects persons as persons, and secures their equal right to live the lives they choose."[10]

Nowhere is this marriage of liberalism's fundamental tenets—state neutrality and individual autonomy—more obvious than in federal jurisprudence, especially in the areas of free speech and privacy. These are complicated areas of the law, but one can perceive a general trajectory in the Court's reasoning that reveals the problematic character of procedural liberalism and suggests its inadequacy in addressing democracy's discontent. Drawing upon Sandel's summary of significant cases, I will of necessity paint with a broad brush here, but let me note that since roughly the 1930s, the Supreme Court has used the 14th Amendment to impose restrictions, such as those found in the Bill of Rights, on state and local governments that were for over a century thought only to apply to the national government. Under this new regime, a variety of statutes and ordinances that could broadly be described as "morals legislation" have failed to pass constitutional muster. Increasingly, the Court has denied local communities and state legislatures the authority to do what had always been thought part and parcel of governance; namely, to secure the conditions for the health, welfare, and morals of the community.

Pursuant to those ends, localities across the country had long-standing restrictions on the production, display, and sale of pornography, based upon the considered judgment that traffic in such goods degraded the community, encouraged vice, and undermined marriage. At one time, the Court recognized the legitimacy of such a judgment. In its *Roth* decision of 1957, the justices reaffirmed traditional legal doctrine denying obscene material constitutional protection and upheld an obscenity conviction on the grounds that the work in question appealed to a "prurient interest."

Beginning in the 1970s, however, the Court came to argue that such reasoning violated state neutrality; if restrictions on pornography were to stand, they would have to be based upon so-called "content neutral" judgments—judgments about material, not moral, harm. For instance, one could no longer ban the presence of an "adult theater" because it would diminish the character of the citizenry or encourage infidelity or damage the moral imagination of children; rather, one would have to appeal to quantifiable, arguably much less important, effects, such as an increase in loitering or a decline in property values. As Chief Justice Burger wrote in *Paris Adult Theatre I v. Slaton* (1973), "The States have the power to make a *morally neutral judgment* that public exhibition of obscene material, or commerce in such material, has a tendency to injure the community as a whole, to endanger the public safety, or to jeopardize . . . the States' 'right to maintain a decent society.'" [11] The same principle was invoked by the Court even more emphatically in *Young v. American Mini Theatres* (1976). Vindicating a Detroit zoning ordinance applied to an "adult theatre," Justice Stevens insisted that the ordinance in question was consistent with "government's paramount obligation of neutrality in its regulation of protected communication." [12] To restrict a pornographic theatre in order to avoid crime or neighborhood deterioration would be a legitimate public purpose; to do so on the basis of moral offense would be illegitimate. Indeed, as Justice Brennan made clear in his *Renton* (1986) opinion, restricting speech in order to protect such goods as the innocence of children or marital fidelity constitutes an "illicit" [13] motive. Only an appeal to secondary effects would be constitutional.

The Court's reliance on secondary effects—typically quantifiable and concrete—for its legitimation of speech ordinances is arguably an adaptation and application of Mill's "harm principle." Exquisitely sensitive to the problem of coercion, Mill insisted in *On Liberty* that "the sole end for which mankind is warranted, individually or collectively, in interfering with the liberty of action of any of their number, is self-protection." As he elaborates, "the *only* purpose for which power can be rightfully exercised over any member of a civilized community, against his will, is to prevent harm to others. His own good, either physical or moral, is not a sufficient warrant." [14] One hears echoes of Mill in the 2002 *Ashcroft* decision in which the Court struck down a federal obscenity statute criminalizing "virtual" child pornography. Among other reasons, the Court argued that because no *actual* children were harmed in the making of the pictures, the pornographic images in question could not be banned; to do so would entail an evaluation of their content. The moral turpitude of the endeavor and the degradation of the agents producing and viewing such material would not suffice to render it unprotected speech. As Sandel helpfully explains, "Insofar as they are justified on moral grounds, restrictions on obscenity violate the liberal principle that law should not embody any particular conception of the good. On the liberal view, it is illegitimate to base laws on judgments about morality and immorality, because to do so violates the principle that government should be neutral among ends. It violates people's 'right to moral independence' by embodying in law a particular theory of the good life and the decent society." The vision of the "unencumbered self" at the heart of political liberalism, he continues, opposes "any view that regards us as obligated to fulfill ends we have not chosen—ends given by nature or God, for example, or by our identities as members of families, peoples, cultures, or traditions."[15]

Sandel rightly questions the validity—and honesty—of this logic. In a line of argument that recalls our earlier discussion of the fragmented university, Sandel prompts us to ask, "Why must we bracket our most deeply held ethical convictions when deliberating about public policy?" Why, for instance, is it constitutional to ground statutes upon what is less important—quantifiable, material things—than on what is more important—the character and soul of a community? In Sandel's words, cannot "communal injury . . . consist in an offense against shared moral standards"?[16] The reflexive response to these questions, one that I encounter among my very bright law students, is the tired canard: law can't impose morality. In a more sophisticated formulation, it goes like this: the state cannot adopt any particular conception of the good, lest it violate individual autonomy.

But, in fact, there is at work here a particular—and controversial, not neutral—conception of the good and a robust set of substantive judgments about the nature of freedom and law. Freedom in this schema is conceived as indeterminate choice, based upon a radically subjective epistemology (that is, an account of how we know what we know). The Court's privacy jurisprudence makes this crystal clear. Let me highlight a 1992 case called *Planned Parenthood v. Casey* to make the point. In order to maintain the nearly unrestricted access to abortion guaranteed by *Roe v. Wade* and its companion *Doe v. Bolton*, the Court's majority offers an account of freedom that will sustain abortion on demand. But it does much more than that, as I will show. "At the heart of liberty," the Justices declare, "is the right to define one's own concept of existence, of meaning, of the universe, and of the mystery of human life. Beliefs about these matters could not define the attributes of personhood were they formed under compulsion of the State." This is a breathtaking endorsement of subjectivism, and I might add that it bears no little resemblance to a certain fateful proposal made in the Garden of Eden. According to the *Casey* Court, *I* define what reality is. *I* define what meaning is. Any law that restricts my choices in intimate matters is illegitimate, because *I* am the arbiter of what is right and what is wrong.

Let me suggest that this quite prevalent understanding of freedom and law—one that undergirds liberalism's tenet of state neutrality—is woefully ill-equipped to address democracy's discontent. If it were consistently applied, it would, in fact, dissolve our political community and render social life chaotic. The discontents surveyed by Sandel could never be ameliorated. Why? Three reasons come immediately to mind. First, because any normative judgment, let alone those that entail legal sanctions, that did not emerge spontaneously from each individual would run afoul of the requirements of autonomy. But autonomy so understood spells the end of the rule of law. Second, as Sandel rightly observes, it also spells the end of those binding ties that are not the product of explicit choice, and this imperils social life, for society rests on many different kinds of bonds that are not voluntarily chosen but are nevertheless binding. (Think, for instance, of the duties we owe to our parents and siblings.) Finally and ironically, the logic of the *Casey* decision would radically undermine the historic, progressive decisions to which this Court considers itself heir, for the enlightened rulings of the Warren era (think, for instance, about *Brown v. Board of Education*) rest upon an objective conception of justice to which we, the citizens, must conform.

Happily, there is a different understanding of freedom and law available in Christian political thought that might well answer the discontents that so vex us. Among the promising features of this alternative is the understanding that politics need not entail a bifurcation of our selves. It need not entail a bracketing of those things we hold most dear. This is because Christian political thought rests upon a fundamentally different anthropology than its liberal rival.

At the heart of this anthropology is not the autonomous, rights-bearing individual, but the person in community, who, having been made in the image and likeness of God, bears the impress of his maker in every dimension of his being. Created by a Trinitarian God, he is intrinsically relational. Interdependence is thus a constitutive, not elective, feature of our existence. And the fundamental duties to which this deep relationality gives rise do not originate in positive law or contracts; they arise naturally in accord with the order of creation.

Importantly, these duties (which might be considered under the rubric of justice) do not diminish us but perfect us. We are, recalling St. Paul, bound and free. We are, like the Israelites of the Exodus, at once liberated and under law. One can make sense of this paradox only by embracing a fundamentally different understanding of freedom than that offered by the liberalism expressed in the *Casey* and *Ashcroft* decisions above.

For the Christian, freedom is not reducible to indeterminate choice; it is much weightier than that. It is the full flourishing of our nature, the perfection of every aspect of our being. It includes in an instrumental sense the power to choose, but this power is only authentically expressed when it chooses the good, that is, when it chooses in accord with what makes us flourish. This is why St. Augustine can describe the saints in heaven as perfectly free, though incapable of sin; blessedly delivered of the false and tawdry counterfeits of the good on offer here, all of their volitional power is rightly directed in the service of love. This is to say that the requirements of the law have found their perfect fulfillment.

In principle, the same holds on earth, though it is only fitfully and imperfectly realized. This surprising claim requires some explanation, for we are used to thinking of freedom and law or autonomy and authority as antinomies. Authority, we are told above, threatens liberty; our modern consciousness immediately associates it with coercion and liberty with spontaneity and choice. Social progress, in consequence, seems to demand an increase in liberty and a proportionate decrease of authority; they are locked in a zero sum game.[17]

Neither the Scriptures nor the orthodox Christian tradition holds this view. Rather, both regard human autonomy as the state of fullest freedom wherein the moral law has been interiorized and guides our decision making definitively. It does not mean that the human subject authors his own moral laws but rather that the person has become an auto-nomos (a self-lawgiver) insofar as he has appropriated and internalized the requirements of the moral law ordained by God for his flourishing. There is a basic connaturality between the human person and the moral order at work here, which overcomes the apparent antinomy of law and freedom.

But autonomy and the happiness that is its end are an achievement, and any human achievement requires cooperation. The quest for autonomy is pursued socially, and the moral law with which autonomy accords concerns not the isolated individual, but the person in community. So, autonomy is essentially related to the common welfare. And to achieve the common welfare requires *political* authority, what the Catholic philosopher Yves Simon calls "a public reason and a public will."[18] Political authority bears an important charge. It is invested by God with the power to determine the requirements of the common good, convey these requirements to the community, and coordinate the activities of individuals and groups so as to achieve this good.

What difference does this make concretely? Let us recall our earlier examples, addressing in general terms the kind of statute deemed illegitimate by liberal jurisprudence. It strikes me that if one's political vision is informed by a Christian understanding of freedom and law, one can readily embrace in principle ordinances that foster a climate of sexual maturity and chastity, as well as laws that protect nascent human life and reinforce the requirements of hospitality incumbent upon any mother. But does this not violate human freedom? No. Because the law is simply removing certain gravely damaging choices that do not in fact lead to human flourishing, which is the very essence of freedom.

Christian political thought thus offers a bracing and radical alternative to the way in which we typically think about politics. Just as a Christian conception of the university recognizes the essential place of theology and philosophy for the proper functioning of the other disciplines, so, too, does a Christian conception of politics recognize the essential place of religious and ethical reflection in matters of public policy and law. In both venues, the academy and the public square, the Christian principles elaborated above promise an integrated vision of the tasks at hand and relieve us of the deepest sources of our discontent. So, whether we are in the classroom or the courtroom, let us be whole persons, thinking and acting in the spirit of Christ, which is to say with love for the world and heaven alike.

Chapter 2 Notes

1. Cited in Francis Martin, *The Feminist Question: Feminist Theology in the Light of Christian Tradition* (Grand Rapids, MI: Eerdmans, 1994), xii.

2. John Henry Newman, *The Idea of a University* (Notre Dame, IN: University of Notre Dame Press, 1990), 50.

3. Niccolo Machiavelli, *The Prince*, trans. Harvey C. Mansfield (Chicago: University of Chicago Press, 1985), 61.

4. Thomas Hobbes, Leviathan (New York: Penguin Books), 160.

5. E. F. Schumacher, *A Guide for the Perplexed* (New York: Harper & Row, 1978), 43.

6. John Paul II, *Evangelium Vitae*, §2.

7. Wendell Berry, "The Loss of the University," in *Home Economics* (New York: North Point, 1987), 82.

8. Michael J. Sandel, *Democracy's Discontent: America in Search of a Public Philosophy* (Cambridge, MA: Belknap Press, 1996), 3. Segments of the analysis of Sandel and Yves Simon have been published in *Christianity and Civil Society: Catholic and Neo-Calvinist Perspectives* (Lanham, MD: Lexington Books, 2008). They have been used here with permission.

9. Sandel, *Democracy's Discontent*, 92.

10. Ibid., 13.

11. *Paris Adult Theatre I v. Slaton*, 413 U.S. 49. As Sandel astutely observes, Burger's "flight from moral judgment" undermines the coherence of his argument. "Allowing the states to decide that commerce in obscenity may 'injure the community as a whole' begs the question whether communal injury can consist in an offense against shared moral standards. If communal injury may not include moral corruption, then why speak of 'the tone of society' rather than crime rates and public safety alone? If communal well-being does include a moral dimension, then why pretend it can be protected by a 'morally neutral judgment'?" (Sandel, *Democracy's Discontent*, 77).

12. *Young v. American Mini Theatres, Inc.*, 427 U.S. 50 (1976).

13. *City of Renton v. Playtime Theatres, Inc.,* 475 U.S. 41 (1986).

14. J.S. Mill, *On Liberty and Other Essays*, ed. John Gray (Oxford: Oxford University Press, 1991), 14 (emphasis added).

15. Sandel, *Democracy's Discontent*, 76, 12.

16. Ibid., 77.

17. Contemporary federal jurisprudence arguably works with the same assumption, as is evident from the discussion above.

18. Yves R. Simon, *Philosophy of Democratic Government* (Notre Dame, IN: University of Notre Dame Press, 1993), 48. Simon illustrates his definition with an example. An army officer has been ordered to hold a certain position. This is the particular good entrusted to him. If he is a good officer, he wills the common good formally; that is to say, he desires the common good (in this case, victory for the whole army) and stands ready to abide its requirements. He does not, however, will the common good materially. He is not in charge of the overall strategy of the campaign; he is not coordinating the various functional units involved in the war effort. He contributes to the common good precisely by attending to the particular good. His general, however, wills the common good formally and materially. He not only desires victory for the army and stands ready to abide its requirements, he actually determines

the requirements of victory, informs his subordinates of their duties in light of the requirements, and coordinates the common action of all the functional units toward their common end.

WHY NO CHRISTIAN SOCIOLOGY?

Exploring the Hidden History of an Interdisciplinary Conversation

John Schmalzbauer[1]

For decades, sociologists have asked, "Why no socialism?" For people of faith, a more pertinent question might be, "Why no Christian sociology?" Compared to the vigor and vitality of Christian scholarship in philosophy and history, such initiatives are strangely absent from the discipline of sociology. The Society of Christian Philosophers currently makes up about one-tenth of the American Philosophical Association, the Conference on Faith and History is celebrating its fortieth anniversary. Both organizations sponsor well-regarded journals and conferences.

Compare this with the portrait Robert Wuthnow painted of a gathering of evangelical sociologists at a conference in New Orleans. Instead of a hotel ballroom, they met in a hotel guestroom for prayer and impromptu communion with crackers and soda. Bound together by warm fellowship, they resembled a small discipleship group more than an academic organization.[2] Consistent with Wuthnow's account, the Christian Sociological Society does not publish a journal or sponsor an annual meeting, confining itself to a newsletter. While the Association of Christians Teaching Sociology sponsors a small conference, it is dominated by faculty at evangelical colleges. Neither organization has the influence of the Society of Christian Philosophers.

And yet there is such a thing as Christian sociology. Over the past century, there have been many focused efforts to bring Christian theology and philosophy into dialogue with sociological perspectives. These include the Social Gospel pieces in the early *American Journal of Sociology*, the quarter-century run of the *American Catholic Sociological Review*, the post-war writings of Peter Berger and Robert Bellah, assorted works of evangelical sociology, the emergence of Radical Orthodoxy, and the revival of philosophical personalism in the social sciences. Many of these initiatives have had significant theological and philosophical content. The problem is that most sociologists have never heard of them, including many people of faith.

To put it bluntly, Christian sociology has a cultural retrievability problem. In "How Culture Works," sociologist Michael Schudson argues that cultural texts and symbols have no efficacy if they cannot be retrieved. Retrievability is all about being in the path of potential audiences.[3] Nearly invisible to most of the academy, the various waves of Christian sociology are easy to avoid. While the early encounter of sociology with the Social Gospel is remembered chiefly by disciplinary historians, the golden era of "Catholic sociology" remains buried in dusty issues of the *American Catholic Sociological Review*, only recently available in electronic form. More recent works on faith and social science are released by religious publishers that few sociologists have heard of.

In its lack of retrievability, Christian sociology is not alone. In both Europe and North America, religious intellectual traditions are becoming harder to retrieve. Sociologist Daniele Hervieu-Leger suggests that the "crumbling of memory" and an ignorance of one's position in a religious lineage is a part of the modern predicament. This is true outside of the academy where many people of faith are unaware of the religious origins of their own beliefs and practices. It is also true in higher education where many scholars have forgotten the Protestant roots of the American university.[4]

Like the wider academy, sociology has experienced a break in its chain of memory, forgetting the influence of religious thought on its origins and development. Noting the presence of Anglican Medievalists and Christian socialists among early British sociologists, John Brewer observes that the "existence of religious sociology has been written out of the history of the discipline in Britain." While distancing itself from historic orthodoxy, early American sociology was shaped by liberal Protestantism and the Social Gospel. Although many prominent sociologists used social science as a weapon against traditional Christianity, secularized Protestant categories made their way into early twentieth-century social theory. This influence parallels the presence of formerly theological concepts in European classical sociology, a lineage explored by John Milbank in *Theology and Social Theory*. Such tacit Protestant categories persisted in the post-war social theory of Talcott Parsons and his students. More recently, some have detected an unacknowledged religious bias in the contemporary sociology of religion, noting the dominance of Christian scholars in this subfield. Others have attributed this "smuggling" to the exclusion of religious arguments from secular discourse, viewing it as a return of the repressed.[5]

In light of these issues, people of faith would benefit from a more reflective discussion of the religious assumptions in social research, assumptions that cross disciplinary boundaries. To advance such a discussion, this chapter analyzes the relationship between sociology and other discourses. First, it offers a historical overview of a century of "Christian sociology," focusing on several discrete episodes when theology and religious philosophy shaped the social sciences. Second, it argues that Christian scholars should be more reflexive about their own theological assumptions, as well as the religious lineage of the field. The two arguments go together. Focusing on the hidden influence of religious ideas, this essay calls attention to the fluidity of disciplinary boundaries. Believing that the future of Christian sociological reflection is in the past, it is also an exercise in sociological *anamnesis*. In an era when the lines between disciplines are increasingly murky, it is important to remember that sociology has always been influenced by other fields. We will begin by considering the influence of theological categories on the founding era of sociology.

Theological Motifs in Early Sociology: Europe and America

In *The Sociological Tradition*, Robert Nisbet celebrates the many neologisms coined in the early decades of the discipline, calling it "one of the richest periods of word formation in history." Along with this new terminology, the masters of European sociology occasionally drew on the vocabulary of Christian theology. While often taking the form of anti-theologies (see the discussion of Milbank below), their writings were shaped by the religious thought of the day. To be sure, early sociologists often turned theology on its head. At the same time, the mere presence of theological terminology, even if deployed for secular ends, is a resource for Christian sociological reflection.[6]

Such language can be found in many of the European classics. In some of the strangest passages in classical sociology, Emile Durkheim uses religious terminology to describe the mysterious relationship between society and the individual. Arguing that "The gods are no other than collective forces personified [*incarnées*] and hypostasized [*hypostasiées*] in material form," he summarizes his theory of religion. Durkheim scholar W. S. F. Pickering notes that hypostasis was once used in the Christological and Trinitarian debates of the patristic period. Though Durkheim uses it to describe the way material objects symbolize the social group, his argument resembles the way theologians talk about the incarnation.[7]

The agnostic son of a rabbi, nobody would confuse Durkheim with a Catholic sociologist. Yet "it is not paradoxical to describe his sociology as Catholic," writes anthropologist Richard Fardon, noting the influence of Catholic conservatives on the thought of Durkheim's predecessors August Comte and Henri Saint-Simon. In making such a claim, Fardon echoes those who have described French positivism as "Catholicism without Christianity."[8] In "Max Weber as 'Christian Sociologist,'" William Swatos makes an even stronger argument about the religious influences on Weberian thought, noting his lifelong involvement with Protestant social reformers and rejection of atheism. From Ernst Troeltsch to H. Richard Niebuhr, Weber's works have served as a resource for Christian theologians. Likewise, Georg Simmel's writings on religion have informed both the theology of Hans Urs von Balthasar and the Catholic sociology of Kieran Flanagan. Finally, philosophers and sociologists have discerned the presence of a "secular eschatology" in the thought of Karl Marx, debating the extent to which theological categories influenced his view of history.[9]

Like its European cousin, early American sociology bears the traces of a religious lineage. Though it is possible to exaggerate this influence, it should not be ignored. As several scholars have documented, many of the discipline's founding fathers were clergy, former clergy, or the children of clergy. Sociologist William Swatos estimates that about one-fifth of the charter members of the American Sociological Society were ordained. At the same time, Swatos notes that only six percent of ASS charter members participated in two early Institutes of Christian Sociology. Though such individuals operated on the edges of the discipline, several key scholars "wore 'Christian sociology' as a hard-earned badge of honor," including Graham Taylor and Charles Henderson. While Taylor used an urban settlement house as his "personal sociological laboratory," Henderson was part of the nation's first real sociology department at the University of Chicago.[10]

Far more influential was the Baptist deacon Albion Small, Henderson's chair and the founding editor of the *American Journal of Sociology*. While distancing himself from "Christian sociology," Small employed overtly religious language to build support for the new field. Though much of this rhetoric was strategic, it reflected a deep immersion in liberal Protestant circles. In his first sociology course at Colby College, Small used the final lecture to call for the establishment of the Kingdom of God. Sociologist Charles Ellwood articulated a similar vision during his years at the University of Missouri, offering a popular course on the "Social Teachings of Jesus." An American Sociological Society president, he published books on *Christianity and Social Science* (1923) and *The World's Need of Christ* (1940). Though these works received mixed reviews, their Christocentric focus reveals much about the early generation of sociologists. Ellwood was not alone. A 1902 listing of social science courses included offerings like "Applied Christianity" and "Sociology from a Christian Point of View."[11]

In *American Sociology: Worldly Rejections of Religion and Their Directions*, Arthur Vidich and Stanford Lyman make much of the influence of Protestantism on early social science, describing a secularized theology that transformed *theodicy* into *sociodicy*. To be sure, many sociologists were fluent in the language of Zion. Echoing St. Paul, Small argued that "men *live and move* and have their being as *members* one of another." Likewise, the young George Herbert Mead predicted that better communication would bring about "the day when everyman will be my neighbor and all life shall be saturated with the divine life." As such quotations suggest, the "theological footprints" of liberal Protestantism can be found within the early publications of American sociology. A century later, it is jarring to read articles by theologians Shailer Matthews and Walter Rauschenbusch in the pages of the *American Journal of Sociology*.[12]

Such religious utterances should not be taken at face value. Early sociologists drank deeply from the secular positivism of August Comte and Herbert Spencer. Like many in the Social Gospel movement, some embraced eugenics, including Charles Ellwood. According to William Swatos, the founders clothed secular ideas in pious language. Rather than creating a Protestant sociology, they invented a "new faith rooted in a particular socio-cultural reading of Judeo-Christian ethics." Sociologist Christian Smith concurs, calling it a "functional equivalent of traditional Christianity."[13]

As Swatos documents in *Faith of the Fathers*, the engagement of sociology with liberal Protestantism was superficial and short lived. Enthralled with quantitative approaches and the rhetoric of positivism, a younger generation rejected the religious agenda of their elders. By the 1930s, the coalition with Protestant reformers had come to an end. After that, religious works by Ellwood and other Social Gospelers were rarely cited (see figure 1). Reflecting a break in the chain of memory, anybody "studying the founders of academic sociology in the United States has the advantage of always finding the treatises written by these figures exactly where they belong on the library shelves."[14]

"Supernatural Sociology" and American Catholicism

In the midst of a secularizing field, at least one major American religious community revived the goal of a distinctively Christian sociology. In 1938, a small band of priest-sociologists, nuns, and lay scholars established the American Catholic Sociological Society. Two years later, the *American Catholic Sociological Review* published its first issue, announcing, "There is such a thing as a Catholic sociology." By 1956, the society had grown to five hundred members.[15]

Like Social Gospel-era liberal Protestantism, mid-century Catholic thought was intertwined with social reform. Proclaiming liturgy "the indispensable basis of social regeneration," Benedictine monk Virgil Michel expressed a communitarian vision of society rooted in Catholic personalism and the mystical body of Christ. Critiquing both capitalism and Marxism, Michel saw the Eucharist as a model for social reconstruction. Influenced by similar theological and philosophical currents, Father Paul Hanly Furfey articulated the need for a "supernatural sociology," arguing that the "existence of the Mystical Body is a socially significant fact and it is just as actual, just as real, just as concrete, as the infant mortality rate of Minnesota in 1939." During the early years of the American Catholic Sociological Society, Furfey and his colleagues explored such topics as "The Individual, the Community, and the Trinity" and "Christian Social Principles." While some members integrated sociology and Catholic social teaching, others favored a clear differentiation of the "roles of social philosopher, social scientist, and social reformer."[16]

On some issues, the society was prophetic. In a period when many social scientists embraced eugenics, Catholic sociologists spoke out against "the development of supermen." Focusing on the background beliefs undergirding all social theory, they also anticipated the reflexive sociology of the 1960s. Believing that "all sociology is colored by social philosophies," Catholic scholars carved out a space for metasociological value judgments. Told that he "sounded like the Catholic sociologists of the mid 1930s," Neo-Marxist sociologist Alvin Gouldner replied, "Indeed I do, and you people should never have given that up."[17]

Gouldner was referring to the assimilation of Catholic sociologists, a process symbolized by the transformation of the *American Catholic Sociological Review* into *Sociological Analysis* and the American Catholic Sociological Society into the Association for the Sociology of Religion. By the early 1970s, such professionalization was nearly complete, as a new generation of "John F. Kennedy Catholic preppies" joined the sociological mainstream. To be sure, not everyone assimilated. While embracing the empiricism of quantitative sociology, Father Andrew Greeley celebrated the "Catholic social ethic" in his studies of religion and ethnicity. Others chose to bracket their religious identities.[18]

Evaluations of mid-century Catholic sociology have been decidedly mixed. At its height, this movement produced very little scholarship, focusing on the task of undergraduate education. In 1952, only 56.7 percent of ACSS members had published a scholarly article or book. Rarely cited by his colleagues, Father Furfey's magnum opus, *The Scope and Method of Sociology* (1953), was ignored by most of the field (see figure 1). Some have criticized his approach on theological grounds. In a 2005 essay, Catholic University sociologist Paul Sullins accused Furfey of misinterpreting the Bible and the church's social encyclicals. By contrast, Notre Dame theologian Michael Baxter has praised him for articulating a social theory "grounded in a Trinitarian understanding of charity."[19]

If nothing else, Catholic sociology offers lessons for other traditions, most notably evangelicalism. Like evangelical Protestants, American Catholics developed a host of scholarly and professional organizations. During its heyday, the American Catholic Sociological Society was the largest academic association dedicated to the integration of Christianity and social science. Nothing since has come close to its size and scope.

Catholic sociologists plied their trade far from the world of sociology's movers and shakers. One exception was the participation of Harvard's Pitirim Sorokin in the 1940 meeting of the American Catholic Sociological Society, where he delivered an address on the crisis of "contemporary sensate culture." The son of an icon painter from northern Russia, he later attributed the mystical bent of his sociological theories to an Eastern Orthodox childhood, noting that the "mysteries of the Agnus Dei, of Creation, Incarnation, Crucifixion, Resurrection, and Redemption as they are so dramatically unfolded in the Russian Orthodox Mass, opened to me the mysteries and enigmatic dimensions of reality and of the tragic aspects of life." This doxological vision came close to the liturgical sensibility of mid-century Catholic sociology. Interpreting society and culture through a sacramental lens, it was a road not taken in American social science.[20]

Mainline Protestantism's Influence on Post-War Sociology

Far more influential was Sorokin's colleague Talcott Parsons, the dominant figure in post-war American sociology. A self-described "backsliding Protestant," Parsons was far from dismissive of Protestantism, carving out a space for religion that reverberated in the work of his students, including Robert Bellah and Clifford Geertz. The son of a Congregational minister, he maintained a lifelong interest in the sacred, an interest that became even more acute in his later years. In "Talcott Parsons, My Teacher," University of Pennyslvania sociologist Renee Fox painted a moving portrait of his inner life, arguing that "Parsons' relationship to symbols and rituals was closely linked to his profound connection to the religious dimensions of human existence."[21]

Parsons wrote at a time when American higher education was undergoing a religious revival. While never an advocate of "Christian sociology," Parsons contributed to an edited volume on *Religious Perspectives in College Teaching*. Funded by the Edward W. Hazen Foundation, it was an effort to promote the integration of faith and learning. Initially dominated by mainline Protestants, the Society for the Scientific Study of Religion (1949) and the Religious Research Association (1951) emerged out of the same cultural milieu. Descended from the Rockefeller-funded Institute for Social and Religious Research (run by the Reverend H. Paul Douglass), the RRA was originally known as the Religious Research Fellowship. The SSSR (then known as the Committee for the Social Scientific Study of Religion) was the product of a Harvard seminar that included Parsons, Sorokin, and theologian Paul Tillich. Its original purpose was to bring "together the social scientist and the religious person." The inaugural issue of the *Journal for the Scientific Study of Religion* was interdisciplinary, including an article by Lutheran philosopher Paul Holmer and a sociological piece on the superiority of the "Judeo-Christian image of man." Written by Carleton College's William Kolb, the latter drew a polite rebuke from Parsons, who argued, "there must be a more generalized, nonpositivistic image of man which can also be Islamic, Buddhist, and Hindu."[22]

This was ironic in light of Parsons' own biases. According to William Buxton, Parsonian sociology was shaped by a "tension between the redemptive impulse of Parsons' liberal Calvinist commitments and the reality of capitalist society." Portraying modern American society as the "virtual endpoint of history," Parsons attributed its rise to Christian individualism and egalitarianism. In *The Coming Crisis of Western Sociology*, Alvin Gouldner uncovered a religious impulse in Parsonian thought, finding a statistical correlation between sociologists' support for functionalism and their own church attendance. Gouldner criticized pious functionalists for ignoring the role of power and conflict in American society.[23]

By contrast, Robert Bellah praised functionalism's "multi-layered and open" view of human social life, citing the work of political scientist Karl Deutsch, who used theological language to describe the "grace" at work in complex social systems. In a recent profile, Michael Lindsay notes that Bellah was trained in the interdisciplinary hothouse of Harvard's Department of Social Relations, "where scholars were busy integrating social scientific research from various fields," including theology. In the preface to *Beyond Belief* (1970), Bellah acknowledged his personal "encounter with the thought of Paul Tillich," adding that *The Courage to Be* "made a deep impression on me." Calling for a reintegration of religion and sociology, Bellah argued that religious symbols are true to the extent they provide meaning and order.[24]

Like Bellah, Peter Berger borrowed heavily from the liberal Protestant tradition. In *The Sacred Canopy* (1969), he articulated the paradigmatic version of the secularization thesis. Written following the "secular city debate" launched by theologian Harvey Cox, it gave sociological expression to "the psychological experience of intellectuals who emerge from religiously conservative families to the religiously indifferent world of the academy." Despite obvious parallels with the religious biographies of mainline Protestant theologians, Berger sharply differentiated his theory from academic theology, embracing a stance of "methodological atheism."[25]

And yet Berger has often served as a religious public intellectual. In *The Noise of Solemn Assemblies* (1961), he excoriated American churches for baptizing the social order. Written before he assumed the role of the detached sociologist, it was part of a wider critique of post-war American religion that found expression in C. Wrights Mills' "A Pagan Sermon to the Christian Clergy" (1958) and Gibson Winter's *The Suburban Captivity of the Churches* (1961). In *A Rumor of Angels* (1970), Berger developed an inductive case for the reality of the supernatural, pointing to such phenomena as humor and play. In *The Heretical Imperative* (1980), he called his readers "back to Schleiermacher," combining sociology with German theology.[26]

Equally at home in the world of theology, Robert Bellah offered a religious interpretation of American nationalism. In *The Broken*

Covenant (1975), he wrote that America's future "depends not only on our action but on grace." Such religious social criticism could also be found in *Habits of the Heart* (1985), a book that lamented the growth of individualism in American life. While not quite theological, it was engaged by many theologians.[27]

While somewhat outside the disciplinary mainstream, the works of Bellah and Berger are among the sociological bestsellers of all time. Their religious writings are an exception to the low visibility of most Christian sociology (see figure 1). According to a 1997 study, *Habits* had sold over 400,000 copies. In 2007, sociologist Michael Lindsay reported that Bellah had been cited in more than 7,000 scholarly articles. According to Lindsay, there are 77 distinct branches of Bellah's intellectual family tree, with 212 active descendants. On a smaller scale, Berger has produced a host of influential graduate students who have gone on to mentor students of their own. Their offspring are among the most perceptive commentators on religion and social life.[28]

How do their works hold up theologically? Some criticize Berger for segregating sociological and religious inquiry, attributing this tendency to the two-kingdom approach of Lutheran theology. Meanwhile, Stanley Hauerwas faults Bellah's *Habits* for presenting a liberal version of the Christian America myth, comparing it to both Jerry Falwell and Walter Rauschenbusch. Along the same lines, theologian John Milbank takes Bellah and Berger to task for confining religion to the margins of society, an approach he calls "policing the sublime." Yet, for the most part, both are well regarded by other Christian scholars. In the words of sociologist David Martin, a priest in the Church of England, Berger has no "doubts about who he is: a Lutheran Rabbi." The same is true of Bellah the Episcopalian. Though neither man created a tradition of Christian sociology, their non-reductionist approach to the discipline created space for others to move in that direction.[29]

Christian Sociology Today: Pro-Religiousness, Radical Orthodoxy, Natural Law

Taking advantage of this space, a growing number of scholars explored what it means to be a Christian sociologist in the 1970s and 1980s. In articles like "Sociological Theory and Religious Truth" and "Toward a Christian Sociological Perspective," they grappled with the writings of Bellah and Berger. Inspired by the critique of value-free social science, they wrote books like *Christians & Sociology* (1975), *Sociology and Theology* (1980), *Looking Both Ways* (1987), and *Social Science in Christian Perspective* (1988). Together, they discussed free will and determinism, structure and agency, and the nature of personhood. Beginning in 1978, the Blackfriars Symposium in Theology and Sociology met for a decade in Oxford. The Christian Sociological Society and the Association of Christians Teaching Sociology were also formed in the 1970s. The Society of Catholic Social Scientists followed in 1992.[30]

Yet if Christian scholars hoped to transform the field through reflections on the integration of faith and learning, they were bound to be disappointed. Though a few of their works were released by major academic presses, most were published by small religious publishers, suggesting the audience for Christian sociology was confined to religious colleges (see figure 1). Many of the authors hailed from the same schools, places not known for their research productivity. In a 1994 survey of thirty-three evangelical institutions, 55 percent of sociology faculty had never published an article in a mainstream journal. Reflecting a similar degree of isolation, the journal of the Society of Catholic Social Scientists is available in just fifty-seven libraries worldwide.[31]

Such low visibility would seem to indicate a decline in the influence of Christian sociologists. Yet elsewhere, others were having an impact. In a 1993 survey conducted by Yale University, 28 percent of sociologists of religion identified as liberal Protestants and 17 percent as evangelicals. Many were Catholic. According to Rodney Stark and Roger Finke, "the most important factor in creating a truly scientific study of religion was the growing participation in it of persons of faith." So strong is the influence of Christianity that some have complained of a pro-religious bias. In "The Emerging Strong Program in the Sociology of Religion," David Smilde and Matthew May argue that pro-religiousness has led to an emphasis on the positive effects of religiosity, as well as a focus on religion as an independent variable. In a follow-up essay, Smilde and three colleagues critique the sub-discipline's Christo-centrism, arguing that in "many past and present sociological studies, 'religion' refers primarily to 'Christianity' and, more specifically, to a narrow range of Christian forms practiced in the United States."[32]

For Christian scholars, this pro-religiousness is a mixed bag. On the one hand, the sacred is no longer marginalized, as researchers document the influence of religion in American society, challenging once-dominant theories of secularization. Yet pro-religious does not always mean openly Christian. Instead of acknowledging the influence of religious commitments, scholars often conceal them, engaging in a form of passive-aggressive Christian sociology. In *The Disenchantment of Secular Discourse*, legal scholar Steven Smith writes that the exclusion of faith from secular discourse leads some to "smuggle" their tacit convictions into scholarly arguments. Such smuggling involves taken-for-granted assumptions and presuppositions which, if made public, "would be controversial: you would have to defend the premise, and you don't want to do that."[33]

Blessed are those who reveal their taken-for-granted assumptions. Yet such candor is not always well received. A case in point is theologian John Milbank's *Theology and Social Theory*, which argues that "'scientific' social theories are themselves theologies or anti-theologies in disguise." Providing a genealogy of sociology's theological roots, it portrays social theory as a Christian heresy. Declaring theology the only true meta-discourse, Milbank advocates "a distinguishable Christian social theory," dubbing it Radical Orthodoxy. Though widely discussed in the humanities, Milbank's proposal has failed to gain traction in the field he has marked for demolition. Ignored by *Contemporary Sociology*, the book has received mixed reviews in other publications. While Catholic sociologist Kieran Flanagan called it a flawed "defence of theology on the basis of an offence on sociology," Robert Wuthnow wrote that Milbank "may be overly harsh."[34]

Despite such criticisms, *Theology and Social Theory* has inspired cross-disciplinary conversations about the place of religious thought across the human sciences. Praising Milbank's alternative view of society and culture, Joel Robbins urged anthropologists to recommit themselves to "finding real otherness in the world." In a special issue of the *South Atlantic Quarterly*, Robbins and Matthew Engelke convened a dialogue between anthropologists and theologians (including Stanley Hauerwas and Catherine Pickstock), exploring the relevance of the biblical Paul to the study of global Christianity. Noting that contemporary philosophers have seen Paul as a "subject committed to radical change," several contributors drew on the work of Slavoj Žižek and Alain Badiou.[35]

Although theology is gaining a fresh hearing in the social sciences, not all Christian scholars advocate an overtly religious approach. Some of the most promising interdisciplinary proposals come from Christian Smith, a sociologist at the University of Notre Dame. In *Moral, Believing Animals*, he argues that human beings cannot be understood apart from their moral and spiritual dimensions. In *What Is a Person? Rethinking Humanity, Social Life, and the Moral Good from the Person Up*, he critiques sociology's treatment of personhood. Though much of the book draws on secular thinkers, he incorporates the insights of philosophical personalism, a tradition with deep roots in the natural law tradition. Conceiving of human beings as persons in relation, rather than isolated individuals, Smith cites a long list of religious thinkers, including the "Polish phenomenologist Karol Wojtyla" (Pope John Paul II), Eastern Orthodox theologian John Zizioulas, and Catholic philosopher Jacques Maritain. In his personalist emphasis on "meeting, sharing, engagement, fellowship, and communion," he echoes some of the themes of mid-century Catholic sociology. While a practicing Catholic, Smith is not proposing an overtly Christian social theory. Instead, he locates his project within critical realism and in natural law theory, a discourse intended to be open to all rational thinkers.[36]

For some, that is not enough. Writing in the *Christian Scholars Review*, philosopher James K. A. Smith criticizes the "timidity" of *What Is a Person?*, noting that its "critical realism turns out to be a sort of nontheistic natural theology." Calling for a more robustly theological approach, he argues that "the *telos* of human personhood is bound up with the person of Christ." Responding to the charge of timidity, Christian Smith notes that most social scientists think that "to believe in the reality of natural law is obviously to be nutters, barking mad, belonging among those interested in hunting witches and fighting Crusades." It remains to be seen what sociologists will make of *What Is a Person?*. The fact that the book was published by the University of Chicago Press should enhance its cultural retrievability.[37]

Conclusion

The debate between Smith and Smith raises a much larger issue: how fluid are the boundaries between sociology and theology? In *People of Faith: Religious Conviction in American Journalism and Higher Education*, I noted that Catholic and evangelical scholars have frequently translated their theological commitments into a form their professional colleagues could understand. Some of the people I interviewed used the language of social justice to connect faith and public policy. Others related discussions about free will and predestination to the structure/agency debate in social theory, seeing a connection between Calvinism and structuralist explanations.[38]

In the sociology of religion, scholars continue to converse with theologians, though such dialogue is often confined to the footnotes. While Nancy Ammerman cites George Lindbeck's *The Nature of Doctrine*, Robert Wuthnow draws on work in narrative theology and the recovery of Christian practices. Though both are careful to distinguish sociology from Christian theology, there is a semi-permeable boundary between the two disciplines. This cross-disciplinary flow of ideas is facilitated by faith-friendly foundations. Over the past two decades, the Lilly Endowment, the John Templeton Foundation, and the Pew Charitable Trusts have funded projects with theological implications. As noted earlier, this privileging of Christian language and assumptions has led to the charge of pro-religiousness. Still, as our brief history of American sociology suggests, such emphases are not new. From the founding fathers to post-war functionalism, the sociological tradition has been haunted by the ghost of liberal Protestant theology.[39]

What are the prospects for interdisciplinary approaches to Christian sociology? With few exceptions, such works have been ignored by the wider discipline. Witness the lack of interest in Kieran Flanagan's provocative *The Enchantment of Sociology* (see figure 1). And yet there are some encouraging developments. At the prestigious Social Science Research Council (established by John D. Rockefeller in 1923), sociologists Craig Calhoun and Jonathan VanAntwerpen have set a place at the table for religious scholars, establishing a program on religion and the public sphere. On the SSRC's Immanent Frame blog, theologians and philosophers have exchanged ideas with sociologists, anthropologists, and literary theorists. Along the same lines, the remarkable visibility of philosopher Charles Taylor's *A Secular Age* has signaled a post-secular phase in the humanities and social sciences (see figure 1). Described by some as a work of Christian apologetics, it narrates the emergence of the secular, as well as the possibilities for religious belief. Likewise, sociologist James Davison Hunter's *To Change the World* is a significant contribution to the conversation between theology and cultural theory.[40]

At the same time, the return of religion in the contemporary social sciences should not blind us to some persistent realities. Disciplinary boundaries are among the most institutionalized features of the modern university. To transgress the sociology/theology divide is to engage in academic heresy. For the foreseeable future, Christian sociologists may have to settle for greater awareness of their interdisciplinary roots. If people of faith cannot bring their commitments to the table, they should at least know how the table was constructed. By cultivating an awareness of sociology's hidden religious lineage, Christian sociologists can be more aware of their own place within the discipline. They can also think creatively about the parallels between theological and sociological categories, parallels that are clearly evident in the history of American social science. Such knowledge may help them learn to sing the songs of Zion in a strange land.

Figure 1: # of Mentions of Key Works of "Christian Sociology" in Selected Academic Journal Databases[41]

Title and Author of Book	Academic OneFile	Academic Search Premie	SocINDEX	JSTOR
Charles Ellwood, *Christianity and Social Science: A Challenge to The Church* (Macmillan, 1923)	0	0	7	24
Charles Ellwood, *The World's Need of Christ* (Abingdon-Cokesbury, 1940)	0	1	11	18
Paul Hanly Furfey, *The Scope and Method of Sociology* (Harper & Brothers, 1953)	2	6	36	23
Peter Berger, *The Noise of Solemn Assemblies* (Doubleday, 1961)	2	13	27	20

Peter Berger, *A Rumor of Angels* (Doubleday, 1969)	22	65	69	65
Robert Bellah, *Beyond Belief* (Harper & Row, 1970)	52	104	162	77
Robert Bellah, et al., *Habits of the Heart* (University of California Press, 1985)	571	1055	877	1072
David Lyon, *Christians and Sociology* (InterVarsity, 1976)	1	2	2	1
David Lyon, *Sociology and the Human Image* (InterVarsity, 1983)	1	5	6	6
David Martin, J.M. Mills, And W.S.F. Pickering, *Sociology and Theology* (Oxford University Press, 1980)	2	7	7	6
Richard Perkins, *Looking Both Ways: Exploring the Interface between Christianity and Sociology* (Baker, 1987)	2	0	0	0
David Fraser & Tony Campolo, *Sociology Through the Eyes of Faith* (HarperCollins, 1992)	0	2	0	0
Kieran Flanagan, *The Enchantment of Sociology: A Study in Theology and Culture* (St. Martin's Press, 1999)	7	10	10	5
John Milbank, *Theology and Social Theory* (Blackwell, 2006)	97	213	38	42
Christian Smith, *Moral, Believing Animals* (Oxford University Press, 2003)	17	36	44	14
Charles Taylor, *A Secular Age* (Harvard University Press, 2007)	128	197	60	19

Chapter 3 Notes

1. Sociologist John Evans commented on an earlier draft of this essay. Missouri State University graduate student Michael Bohlen provided valuable assistance.

2. Robert Wuthnow, "Living the Question: Evangelical Christianity and Critical Thought," *CrossCurrents*, Summer 1990, www.crosscurrents.org/wuthnow.htm.

3. Michael Schudson, "How Culture Works: Perspectives from Media Studies on the Efficacy of Symbols," *Theory and Society* 18.2 (1989): 153-180.

4. Daniele Hervieu-Leger, *Religion as a Chain of Memory* (New Brunswick, NJ: Rutgers University Press, 2000). On Protestantism's forgotten influence on higher education, see John Schmalzbauer, "Searching for Protestantism in the *Encyclopedia of Protestantism*," *Religion* 35.4 (2005): 247-265.

5. John D. Brewer, "Sociology and Theology Reconsidered: Religious Sociology and the Sociology of Religion in Britain," *History of the Human Sciences* 20.2 (2007): 7-28; John Milbank, *Theology and Social Theory* (London: Blackwell, 2003). On religious bias, see David Smilde and Matthew May, "The Emerging Strong Program in the Sociology of Religion," SSRC Working Papers, 8 February 2010 http://blogs.ssrc.org/tif/wp-content/uploads/2010/02/Emerging-Strong-Program-TIF.pdf. The "smuggling" argument comes from Steven D. Smith, *The Disenchantment of Secular Discourse* (Cambridge, MA: Harvard University Press, 2010).

6. Robert Nisbet, *The Sociological Tradition* (New York: Basic Books, 1966), 23.

7. Durkheim quoted in Bryan S. Turner, Preface to Emile Durkheim, *Professional Ethics and Civic Morals* (New York: Routledge, 1992), xxxvii; W. S. F. Pickering, *Durkheim's Sociology of Religion: Themes and Theories* (London: Routledge & Kegan Paul, 1984).

8. Richard Farnon, *Mary Douglas: An Intellectual Biography* (New York: Routledge, 1999), 247-248.

9. William Swatos, "Max Weber as 'Christian Sociologist,'" *Journal for the Scientific Study of Religion* 30.4 (1991): 347-362; Kieran Flanagan, "The Return of Theology: Sociology's Distant Relative," in *The Blackwell Companion to Sociology of Religion*, ed. Richard Fenn (Malden, MA: Blackwell, 2001), 432-444; Robert C. Tucker, *Philosophy and Myth in Karl Marx* (Cambridge, UK: Cambridge University Press, 1961).

10. See S. E. Henking, "Sociological Christianity and Christian Sociology: The Paradox of Early American Sociology," *Religion and American Culture* 3.1 (1993): 49-67; William Swatos, "The Faith of the Fathers: On the Christianity of Early American Sociology," *Sociological Analysis* 44.1 (1983): 32-53. Statistics on clergy sociologists can be found in Swatos, "Religious Sociology and the Sociology of Religion in America at the Turn of the Century: Divergences from a Common Theme," *Sociological Analysis* 50.4 (1989): 366-367. The quotes are from Gary Dorrien, *Social Ethics in the Making: Interpreting an American Tradition* (Malden, MA: Blackwell, 2009), 36, 43.

11. On Small, see Swatos, "The Faith of the Founders," 32-53; Christian Smith, "Secularizing American Higher Education: The Case of Early American Sociology," in *The Secular Revolution: Power, Interests, and Conflict in the Secularization of American Public Life*, ed. Christian Smith (Berkeley, CA: University of California Press, 2003), 97-159. The reference to Small's lecture is from Dorothy Ross, *The Origins of American Social Science* (Cambridge, UK: Cambridge University Press, 1991), 124. On Ellwood, see Stephen Turner, "Charles Ellwood and the Division of Sociology," in *Sociology in*

America: A History, ed. Craig Calhoun (Chicago: University of Chicago Press, 2007), 115-154. Course titles are taken from Myer S. Reed, "An Alliance for Progress: The Early Years of the Sociology of Religion in the United States," *Sociological Analysis* 42.1 (1981): 41.

12. Arthur J. Vidich and Stanford M. Lyman, *American Sociology: Worldly Rejections of Religion and Their Directions* (New Haven, CT: Yale University Press, 1987); Albion Small, *General Sociology* (Chicago: University of Chicago Press, 1905), 208. Mead quoted in Ross, *The Origins of American Social Science*, 169. The phrase "theological footprints" comes from Richard Blake, *Afterimage: The Indelible Catholic Imagination of Six American Filmmakers* (Chicago: Loyola Press, 2000), 13.

13. Christine Rosen, *Preaching Eugenics: Religious Leaders and the American Eugenics Movement* (New York: Oxford University Press, 2004); Swatos, "The Faith of the Fathers," 35; Smith, *The Secular Revolution*, 126.

14. William Swatos, *Faith of the Fathers: Science, Religion, and Reform in the Development of Early American Sociology* (Bristol, IN: Wyndham Hall Press, 1984). See also Myer S. Reed, "After the Alliance: The Sociology of Religion in the United States from 1925 to 1949," *Sociological Analysis* 43.3 (1982): 189-204. The quote is from Daniel Breslau, "The American Spencerians: Theorizing a New Science," in *Sociology in America: A History*, ed. Craig Calhoun (Chicago: University of Chicago Press, 2007), 39.

15. See Peter Kivisto, "The Brief Career of Catholic Sociology," *Sociological Analysis* 50.4 (1989): 351-361. Membership data can be found in Loretta Morris, "Secular Transcendence: From ACSS to ASR," *Sociological Analysis* 50.4 (1989): 329-349. The quote is from Raymond Murray, "Presidential Address," *American Catholic Sociological Review* 1.1 (1940): 39.

16. The Michel quote is from Mark and Louise Zwick, *The Catholic Worker Movement: Intellectual and Spiritual Origins* (Mahwah, NJ: Paulist Press, 2005), 59. On Furfey, see Eugene McCarraher, "The Church Irrelevant: Paul Hanly Furfey and the Fortunes of American Catholic Radicalism," *Religion and American Culture* 7.2 (1997): 163-194. The mystical body quote is from Furfey, "Why a Supernatural Sociology?," *American Catholic Sociological Review* 1.4 (1940): 167. A list of research interests can be found in Marguerite Reuss, "1940 Research Census of Members of the American Catholic Sociological Society," *American Catholic Sociological Review* 1.4 (1940): 192-197. On the differentiation of roles, see Kivisto, "The Brief Career of Catholic Sociology," 357.

17. Paul J. Mundie, "The Family in Transition," *American Catholic Sociological Review* 2.1 (1941): 42. The quote about social philosophies is from Murray, "Presidential Address," 42. Gouldner quoted in Joseph P. Fitzpatrick, "Catholic Sociology Revisited: The Challenge of Alvin Gouldner," *Thought* 53.209 (1978): 124.

18. The JFK Preppies reference is from Joseph Varacalli, "Catholic Sociology in America: A Comment on the Fiftieth Anniversary Issue of Sociological Analysis," *International Journal of Politics, Culture, and Society* 4.2 (1990): 251. On Greeley, see John Schmalzbauer, *People of Faith: Religious Conviction in American Journalism and Higher Education* (Ithaca, NY: Cornell University Press, 2003).

19. Thomas J. Harte, "Catholics as Sociologists," *American Catholic Sociological Review* 13.1 (1952): 8; Paul Sullins, "Paul Hanly Furfey and the Catholic Intellectual Tradition," in *Paul Hanly Furfey's Quest for a Good Society*, eds. Bronislaw Misztal,

Francesco Villa, and Eric Sean Williams (Washington, D.C.: Council for Research in Values and Philosophy, 2005), http://www.crvp.org/book/Series01/I-32/chapter-8. htm; Michael J. Baxter, "From Weber and Aristotle and Beyond: The Journey of a Catholic Sociologist," *Catholic Social Science Review* 3.1 (1998): 25

20. Pitirim Sorokin, "Tragic Dualism, Chaotic Syncretism, Quantitative Colossalism, and Diminishing Creativeness of the Contemporary Sensate Culture," *American Catholic Sociological Review* 1.2 (1941): 3-22; Sorokin, *A Long Journey: The Autobiography of Pitirim A. Sorokin* (New Haven, CT: College and University Press, 1963), 40. Beginning in 1946, Sorokin's work was generously supported by the philanthropist Eli Lilly. Despite this patronage, his impact on the field was modest. See James H. Madison, *Eli Lilly: A Life, 1885-1977* (Bloomington, IN: Indiana Historical Society, 1989), 193-197.

21. Renee Fox, "Talcott Parsons, My Teacher," *American Scholar* 66.3 (1997): 405.

22. Douglas Sloan, *Faith and Knowledge: Mainline Protestantism and Higher Education* (Louisville, KY: Westminster John Knox Press, 1994); Talcott Parsons, "Religious Perspectives in College Teaching: Sociology and Social Psychology," in, *Religious Perspectives in College Teaching,* ed. Hoxie Fairchild (New York: Ronald Press, 1952), 286-337. On the early SSSR and RRA, see James Gilbert, *Redeeming Culture: American Religion in an Age of Science* (Chicago: University of Chicago Press, 1997), 253-271; William Swatos, "Religious Research Association," in Swatos and Peter Kivisto, eds., *Encyclopedia of Religion and Society* (Walnut Creek, CA: AltaMira Press, 1998), 408-409. The goals statement from SSSR organizer J. Paul Williams appears on page 256. On the Harvard seminar, see Rodney Stark and Roger Finke, *Acts of Faith: Explaining the Human Side of Religion* (Berkeley, CA: University of California Press, 2000), 16. See also Paul Holmer, "Scientific Language and the Language of Religion," *Journal for the Scientific Study of Religion* 1.1 (1961): 42-60; William Kolb, "Images of Man in the Sociology of Religion," *Journal for the Scientific Study of Religion* 1.1 (1961): 5-29; Talcott Parsons, "Comment," *Journal for the Scientific Study of Religion* 1.1 (1961): 28.

23. William Buxton, *Talcott Parsons and the Capitalist Nation-State* (Toronto: University of Toronto Press, 1985), 12. The endpoint quote is from Steven Seidman, *Contested Knowledge: Social Theory Today* (Malden, MA: Wiley-Blackwell, 2004), 77. The survey findings are from Gouldner, *The Coming Crisis of Western Sociology* (New York: Basic Books, 1970), 258.

24. Robert Bellah, *Beyond Belief: Essays on Religion in a Post-Traditional World* (Berkeley, CA: University of California Press, 1991[1970]), 241, xv; Karl Deutsch, *The Nerves of Government* (New York: Free Press, 1966); Michael Lindsay, "Good Habits of Mind," *Commonweal* (6 April 2007), http://findarticles.com/p/articles/mi_m1252/is_7_134/ai_n27216842/.

25. Peter Berger, *The Sacred Canopy: Elements of a Sociological Theory of Religion* (Garden City, NY: Doubleday, 1969); Harvey Cox, *The Secular City* (New York: Macmillan, 1965); Daniel Callahan, ed., *The Secular City Debate* (New York: Macmillan, 1966). The quote is from R. Stephen Warner, "Work in Progress Toward a New Paradigm for the Sociological Study of Religion in the United States," *American Journal of Sociology* 98.5 (1993): 1044-1093.

26. Peter Berger, *The Noise of Solemn Assemblies: Christian Commitment and the Religious Establishment in America* (Garden City, NY: Doubleday, 1961); Gibson

Winter, *The Suburban Captivity of the Churches: An Analysis of Protestant Responsibility in the Expanding Metropolis* (Garden City, NY: Doubleday, 1961). On Mills' sermon, see Dan Wakefield, "Taking It Big: The Spiritual Legacy of C. Wright Mills" on Beliefnet, http://www.beliefnet.com/Faiths/2000/12/Taking-It-Big.aspx. See also Berger, *A Rumor of Angels: Modern Society and the Rediscovery of the Supernatural* (Garden City, NY: Doubleday, 1970); Berger, *The Heretical Imperative: Contemporary Possibilities of Religious Affirmation* (Garden City, NY: Doubleday, 1979), 116.

27. Robert Bellah, *The Broken Covenant: American Civil Religion in Time of Trial* (Chicago: University of Chicago Press, 1975), 163; Robert Bellah, Richard Madsen, William M. Sullivan, Ann *Swidler,* and Steven M. Tipton, *Habits of the Heart: Individualism and Commitment in American Life* (Berkeley, CA: University of California Press, 1985). For theological reactions to *Habits,* see Charles Reynolds, ed., *Community in America: The Challenge of Habits of the Heart* (Berkeley: University of California Press, 1988).

28. Herbert Gans, "Best-Sellers by Sociologists: An Exploratory Study," *Contemporary Sociology* 26.2 (1997): 131-135; Michael Lindsay, "How Bellah's Ideas Spread: The Diffusion of a Scholar's Influence," *ASA Footnotes* (May/June 2007), http://www.asanet.org/footnotes/mayjun07/fn15.html.

29. Joseph Varacalli, "Neo-Orthodoxy, the Crisis of Authority, and the Future of the Catholic Church in the United States," *Faith & Reason* (Fall 1989), http://www.ewtn.com/library/CHRIST/FR89203.TXT; Stanley Hauerwas, "A Christian Critique of Christian America," in *Community in America,* ed. Charles Reynolds, 250-265; Milbank, *Theology and Social Theory,* 101-143; David Martin, "Berger: An Appreciation," in *Peter Berger and the Study of Religion,* ed. Linda Woodhead with Peter Heelas and David Martin (London: Routledge, 2001), 15.

30. Benton Johnson, "Sociological Theory and Religious Truth," *Sociological Analysis* 38.4 (1977): 368-388; Margaret Poloma, "Toward a Christian Sociological Perspective," *Sociological Analysis* 43.2 (1982): 95-108; David Lyon, *Christians and Sociology* (Downers Grove, IL: InterVarsity Press, 1975); David Martin, John Orme Mills, and W. S. F. Pickering, *Sociology and Theology: Alliance and Conflict* (Brighton, UK: Harvester Press, 1980); Richard Perkins, *Looking Both Ways: Exploring the Interface Between Christianity and Sociology* (Grand Rapids, MI: Baker Book House, 1987); Paul Marshall and Robert E. VanderVennen, *Social Science in Christian Perspective* (Lanham, MD: University Press of America, 1988); Brewer, "Sociology and Theology Reconsidered," 23.

31. Robert W. Fagan and Raymond G. DeVries, "The Practice of Sociology at Christian Liberal Arts Colleges," *American Sociologist* 25.2 (1994): 21-39. The journal statistic is taken from WorldCat.

32. Harry S. Stout and Robert M. Taylor, Jr., "Studies of Religion in American Society: The State of the Art," in *New Directions in American Religious History,* eds. Harry S. Stout and D. G. Hart (New York: Oxford University Press, 1997), 21; Roger Finke and Rodney Stark, *Acts of Faith: Explaining the Human Side of Religion* (Berkeley, CA: University of California Press, 2000), 15; Smilde and May, "The Emerging Strong Program in the Sociology of Religion," http://blogs.ssrc.org/tif/wp-content/uploads/2010/02/Emerging-Strong-Program-TIF.pdf; Peggy Levitt, Courtney Bender, Wendy Cadge, and David Smilde, "Toward a New

Sociology of Religion," The Immanent Frame, http://blogs.ssrc.org/tif/2010/02/15/new-sociology-of-religion/.

33. Smith, *The Disenchantment of Secular Discourse*, 36.

34. Milbank, *Theology and Social Theory*, 3, 382; Kieran Flanagan, "Theology and Social Theory," *British Journal of Sociology* 44.2 (1993): 360-361; Robert Wuthnow, "Is There a Place for 'Scientific' Studies of Religion," *Chronicle of Higher Education*, 24 (January 2003): B10-B11.

35. Joel Robbins, "Anthropology and Theology: An Awkward Relationship," *Anthropological Quarterly* 79.2 (2006): 285-294; Joel Robbins and Matthew Engelke, "Introduction," *South Atlantic Quarterly* 109.4 (2010): 625. The entire issue is available at http://saq.dukejournals.org/cgi/reprint/109/4/.

36. Christian Smith, *What Is a Person? Rethinking Humanity, Social Life, and Moral Good from the Person Up* (Chicago: University of Chicago Press, 2010), 99, 73.

37. James K. A. Smith, "The (Re)Turn to the Person in Contemporary Theory," *Christian Scholars Review* 40.1 (2010): 87, 79; Christian Smith, "More Realism, Critically," *Christian Scholars Review* 40.2 (2011): 209.

38. Schmalzbauer, *People of Faith*, 81, 171-176.

39. Nancy Ammerman, *Congregation and Community* (New Brunswick, NJ: Rutgers University Press, 1997), 393, 431; Robert Wuthnow, *Christianity in the Twenty-First Century: Reflections on the Challenges Ahead* (New York: Oxford University Press, 1995), 49, 224; Robert Wuthnow, *After Heaven: Spirituality in America Since the 1950s* (Berkeley, CA: University of California Press, 2000), 245. The ghost reference is a loose paraphrase of Russell McCutcheon's observation that "the ghost of Paul Tillich yet haunts the field" of religious studies in *Critics not Caretakers: Redescribing the Public Study of Religion* (Albany, NY: SUNY Press, 2001), 180.

40. Kieran Flanagan, *The Enchantment of Sociology: A Study of Theology and Culture* (New York: Macmillan, 1999). The SSRC's Immanent Frame blog can be found at http://blogs.ssrc.org/tif/; Charles Taylor, *A Secular Age* (Cambridge, MA: Harvard University Press, 2007); James Davison Hunter, *To Change the World: The Irony, Tragedy, and Possibility of Christianity in the Late Modern World* (New York: Oxford University Press, 2010).

41. These counts reflect searches conducted by Michael Bohlen and John Schmalzbauer at Missouri State University in late 2010 and early 2011. The number of journal titles available under JSTOR and other databases varies by university, depending on which packages the institution has purchased. The numbers in this table offer a rough indication of the visibility of each text.

ENGLISH BEYOND INTEGRATION

David Lyle Jeffrey

The relationship between the content of Christian faith and the content and practices of English Literature as a university discipline is complex historically and freighted with ironies. In many respects these ironies persist into the postmodern era, characterizing what now appears to be a recurrence of an initial crisis of identity thought once to have been overcome in the nineteenth century. Moreover, as the disciplines of vernacular literary study seem now to face an uncertain future, these originary ironies (perhaps it might be better to think of them as unresolved contradictions) continue to determine key questions that the discipline, I would argue, must answer rather creatively if it is to maintain a continued place of prominence in the academy. Recently, dominant secularist ideologies have come to bear heavily upon the way questions about basic identity and social purpose, practical utility as well as philosophical merit, are now posed and, most especially, answered. Perhaps among the most pressing of current challenges for English Literature are those arising from the postmodern shift in focus from the literature itself to ideological advocacies of one kind or another; these inevitably involve questions about the character and value of the contribution of literary studies to related university disciplines such as History, Philosophy, Classics, Theology, and the Fine Arts.

My purpose in these pages is to be diagnostic, and that, as Chaucer would say, "in litel space"; it is not to attempt an apologia for the discipline. There are many things to say about redemptive developments in various quarters, and I have elsewhere been only too glad to be among those praising achievements which have seemed evidently deserving of it.[1] But our task here is critical assessment, in a time of cultural and economic crisis, both to raise essentially clinical questions about the present health of the discipline and also to consider regimens of physic such as might extend its useful life, even perhaps renew it in health and vigor. Sentimentality or flattery is not at this point likely to be very helpful. To accomplish my purpose I must in fact risk what may seem indignity to the patient.

English Literature as a University Discipline: A Brief History

In this regard it is important to reflect upon the establishment of English as a university discipline in the nineteenth century, in particular with the introduction of English Literature into the university curriculum at Oxford University.[2] Notably, the case for English Literature at Oxford was then formulated in part out of a nationalistic sense that the inherent excellence of vernacular literature in Britain had become somehow comparable to that of ancient Greece and Rome. Nationalism was later to become a factor in the establishment of vernacular literary studies in the American curriculum as well, and the pattern was repeated in the former British colonies around the world. But from the time that Matthew Arnold became the first holder of the Chair of Poetry at Oxford to teach vernacular English rather than Latin and Greek poetry exclusively (1857), one can readily discern another motive, namely a considered *rejection* of the perceived tacit integration of Christian thought in the wider humanistic disciplines.[3] On the one hand, Christian worldview— or at least what was felt by some to be a too-pervasive imprint upon all university study of the Established Church—could be characterized as the result of a persistence of Theology as a formal discipline alongside such disciplines as the study of Classical Literature and Oriental Studies such that Theology unduly co-opted these disciplines through a kind of contamination. (Many of the undergraduate students were Anglican prebends or ordinands.) But on the other hand, in the dominant English literary foundations (e.g., Shakespeare, Milton, and the English Bible), the self-evidently Christian content and cultural presupposition of the vernacular canon now suddenly opened up for formal study provided Arnold and others with a moralistic argument for the study of English literature as a kind of substitute ethical formation for a new age. This apologetic served both to diffuse and, to some degree, disguise the original impulse to secularize. Complexity engendered complicity. For example, it necessitated a rhetorical camouflage to disguise the obvious real shift in worldview from Christian to secular. Many practitioners remained for the totality of their careers essentially confused about the ontology of the modern discipline, believing all the while that sufficient justification had been made for the preeminence of English Literature as a source of moral formation and a guardian of national identity. Others—and Arnold was first among them—saw that there would be a need for further justificatory theory for the discipline which would preserve its claim to moral authority without obliging it too much to residual norms of Christian doctrine. Diplomatically, this required a redefinition of the element of faith itself as a secular cultural property, and to this task of redefinition the earliest proponents of the discipline directed considerable energy.

But, as literature in the time of the Edwardian decadence and early modernism drew attention to itself almost in proportion to its capacity to thwart normative Victorian conceptions of Christian doctrine and scandalize the guardians of public morality (one may think here of reaction to the life and works of Thomas Hardy, Oscar Wilde, James Joyce, the Bloomsbury group, and D. H. Lawrence), the need for alternative theoretical justification became increasingly obvious. It was equally clear to those who took up that task that the grounds of such justification could no longer be based on the claim to provide a moral formation for the young. Subsequently, we may identify three broad stages in the evolution of defenses or apologia for English Literature.

The first of these was a spirited effort to argue for the role of literature as a revolutionary art form, part of the necessary dialectical development of proletarian values and secular resistance to old hegemonies. This is the stance reflected in the essays of Karl Marx and the literary apologetics of Fabian socialism as represented by George Bernard Shaw. In America, the arguments of literary naturalists influenced by Emile Zola and the positivists generally held sway, enriched by Marxist ideas, in particular in the work of Theodore Dreiser, Stephen Crane, John Steinbeck, Upton Sinclair, and Carl Sandburg.[4] In various exemplars of this movement on both sides of the Atlantic, it is evident that socialist worldviews of one sort or another had effectively been exchanged for earlier Christian presuppositions.

The second stage was in part a reaction to the first, that is, to the overt politicization of the socialists, and it may be thought of as a retreat into political disinterestedness obtained in part by a new aestheticism. Among advocates of a less political rationale for literary study (in America, the New Critics under Cleanth Brooks, Alan Tate, and Robert Penn Warren were important leaders in this regard), the formal properties of literature were taken to be the most legitimate focus for study in the university context, and it was argued that, to as great a degree as possible, worldview considerations should be excluded from the analysis of literary texts so that their architectonic and stylistic attributes might receive a kind of "value-free" consideration. A famous articulation of the basic principle is Archibald MacLeish's contention that a poem "should not mean but be."[5]

The third stage is a reaction against the second, and only secondarily an attempt to revive and give selective local application to the principles of the socialists. Here the story becomes much more complex than can be recounted in adequate detail, and footnoted references must serve to indicate even the barest outline of the scope and industry of the practitioners. Their most recent and still current professionalization of the discipline has come about in the context of a much more radically fragmented and contentious postmodern competition of advocacies. Though there is a common stem for most of the contemporary postmodern movements, in part to be identified with the emergence of the structuralism of Roland Barthes and others as a formalism pure enough to demand the "death of the author" as a precondition for literary criticism, the linguistic indeterminism of Saussure and others implied a new subjectivism so radical as to preclude the possibility of any universal or even commensurable discourse. The cacophony of competing and mutually exclusive theories has produced what one critic has called *The Zeitgeist in Babel*.[6] Yet for the purposes of our general understanding, there are evident commonalities: neo-Freudian, Lacanian, Foucauldian, Jungian, Derridean deconstructionist, gender feminist, queer theorist, and other forms of "post-structuralist" appropriations of the literary classroom all agree with the Marxists, and against the formalists, that worldview matters. And yet, paradoxically, they also agree that there is no place in the curriculum for texts which claim a foundational, let alone a revelatory, status and that traditional religion of a text-based kind is invariably an enemy of the rights of individuals and groups to create their own truths and identity-bearing texts as social constructs. All literature on such a view is inherently political, and therefore constitutively antagonistic to authority not its own. Jonathan Culler would claim that literary theory in this disposition becomes "an essentially anti-theological activity," and Jacques Derrrida that the postmodern critic is opposed inevitably to "logocentric" [i.e., Christian] tradition in a fashion that must "*necessarily* take the form of a struggle to the death . . . without any possibility of reconciliation or mediation."[7] Ironically, the intensity of such antagonism made the older Marxists and Christians seem to have more in common with each other than they might otherwise have thought; traditional Marxists like Terry Eagleton (*After Theory*) would later part company with most postmodernist-poststructuralist approaches to the degree that the advocacies advanced had now lost any claim to universal principles for social change and consequently, Eagleton believed, fragmented the otherwise irresistible social force that Marxism ought, especially in the wake of a faded Christianity, to have become.[8] When Jean-François Lyotard described postmodernism as implying the death of all meta-narratives, Marxism was certainly one of the two grand narratives he had in mind[9]; some of the more recent work in literary theory can surely be regarded as a post-Marxian as well as a post-Christian phenomenon.

The earlier grand narrative for literature in the West after the decline and fall of Rome had been, of course, that provided by the Bible and biblical tradition. Certainly until the time of Arnold and the establishment of vernacular literary study as a university discipline parallel to Classics, this meta-narrative was the dominant matrix for literary creation and, in its development, it had enabled redemption and integration of pagan learning as part of its own intertextual fabric.[10] The English literary curriculum which came into being in the late nineteenth and early twentieth centuries was in fact so indebted to biblical (as well as classical) literature that it did not occur to figures such as Arnold or even T. S. Eliot that the discipline could be intelligently studied apart from a prerequisite familiarity with the Bible as a foundation. Arnold argued accordingly for formal inclusion of the Bible as literature (rather than as religion) in the curriculum.[11] If Eliot was later to query this, it was not because he doubted the necessity of the foundation but rather that he doubted the intelligibility of Arnold's attempt to preserve the Bible as if it was to be regarded simply as literature. For Eliot, this was to misconstrue the character of its influence as meta-narrative for English literary history: "The Bible," he insists, "has had a literary influence *not* because it has been considered as literature but because it has been considered as the report of the Word of God."[12] C. S. Lewis was likeminded: "Unless the *religious* claims of the Bible are again acknowledged, its literary claims will … be given only 'mouth honour,' and that decreasingly."[13] What Christian intellectuals such as Eliot and Lewis could see clearly is that any attempt to comprehend the formative power and pervasive influence of the Bible upon literature without attempting first to comprehend the transcendent imagination that gave rise to the production and transmission of biblical literature was doomed to incoherence.

Yet not only was the separation of literature from its ontological sources to win out in one critical method after another, by the end of the twentieth century there would be a principled effort to expunge from the literary canon itself those works which more or less incorrigibly bore witness to a centuries-old integration of faith and the literary imagination. Within the last quarter century, not only the earliest English (Anglo-Saxon) literature, but landmark epics such as Milton's *Paradise Lost* and Spenser's *Faerie Queene*, the religious heart and sermonic conclusion of Chaucer's *Canterbury Tales*, many of Shakespeare's plays, the poetry of Donne, Herbert, and their contemporaries have tended to be optional if available at all. More recently, the works of Eliot, Lewis, and J. R. R. Tolkien—not only their fiction and poetry but also their critical writing—have likewise been exiled to the margins of the English curriculum if not banished altogether. Much of this has been done in the name of cultural diversity, but in fact the sheer loss of cultural memory of the biblical foundations has produced more than sufficient excuse for curricular revision all by itself. When it takes two pages of annotation to render one page of Eliot intelligible, one has reached a point of diminishing returns.

The resulting curricular deformation, however, adds irony to irony. Many of the greatest works of English literature, such as in their *gravitas* once made a plausible case for the intellectual probity of English among the disciplines, have been replaced by shallow contemporary works of dubious merit, and justifications for their study in place of the "greats" have been based on fractional social agendas largely unrelated to any concern for the intellectual merits of the discipline. One consequence of canonical diminishment alongside attempted trendiness has been a reduction in the number of students following the undergraduate major[14]; another has been a decline in the public authority and especially the "moral high ground" for the discipline which, until the 1960s, had been still earnestly advocated by figures such as Northrop Frye, Maynard Mack, and Lionel Trilling. Not less damaging than these losses has been their proximate cause, namely degeneration of the concept of intellectual community within departments of English generally[15] and a subsequent loss of prestige extra-departmentally among the humanities disciplines among which, at one time, English would have been seen as a leader. Already more than a decade ago, major scholars were publishing critiques and calls to arms regarding these matters in weighty and worthy volumes: Carl Woodring's *Literature, an Embattled Profession* (Columbia University Press, 1999), Alvin Kernan's *What Happened to the Humanities?* (Princeton University Press, 1997), Robert Scholes' *The Rise and Fall of English* (Yale University Press, 1998), John Ellis' *Literature Lost: Social Agendas and the Corruption of the Humanities* (Yale University Press, 1997), and Michael Berube's *The Employment of English: Theory, Jobs and the Future of Literary Studies* (New York University Press, 1997) are only a few of these, but the titles as well as the caliber of both authors and presses indicate the prominence with which the warning was being sounded. Yet in the secular universities almost nothing has changed in the intervening years.

To summarize the historical context: preservation of intellectual *gravitas* sufficient to constitute English literature as a discipline comparable to disciplines such as Classics, Philosophy, and History has not been possible given the evolution of postmodern literary study. In an attempted prophylaxis against the intrinsic religious content of great works in the English canon, as well as a corresponding attempt to market the discipline competitively as one among many species of entertainment or social statement, the case for English as a discipline comparable in intellectual value to the literature of Greece, Rome, and perhaps the Bible, has become increasingly unconvincing to those who most must be convinced by it—students, academics, and the guardians of the public purse.

Future Choices

Like many of the academic disciplines introduced in the nineteenth century then, it seems that English Literature, in the wake of postmodernism, has come to something of an *aporia*—or, if that seems too strong a term, at least to a logical impasse. Although much of our current effort at any moment is of contemporary interest and topical value, an evident gap has opened up between the historical, textual, and intellectual resources of the discipline and the fashionable preoccupations of contemporary critical practice. This gap has led to curricular incoherence and often, according to many observers, an intellectual ephemerality such that the academic culture of the discipline has become notorious. Increasingly, we are known less for high rhetoric, intellectual profundity, and admirable critical insight than for rhetorical obscurantism, jejune carnality, and a loss of capacity even to distinguish between good and bad writing. These factors pose critical questions for the future of the discipline, even as, unfortunately, they tend to cloud the judgment of those who must inevitably make the formative decisions. Each of these *problematiques* pertain directly to some aspect of the *status quo ante*.

First: in light of the decline of the discipline already evident in the secular universities, and of the radical diminution of the canon—effectively in a context in which the erasure of cultural memory has been a key strategy of some theorists—one pressing question concerns the preservation of cultural memory. How may we keep the memory of great works of literary art alive and interactive with present consciousness? This question pertains not only to the readability of Chaucer, Shakespeare, and Milton, but also to the viability for future study of nearly all of our prominent "canonical" authors.

Here, one should note, the advantages of the smaller liberal arts college with a still-living Christian tradition are many. The secular university, state-funded and proscriptively pluralist, has by this point an irrefragable investment in the *status quo ante* of an etiolated public high school curriculum, the trivializing economies of capitalist advertising, and what Neil Postman once called "amusing ourselves to death," namely the televised anesthetics to reflective thinking issued by the gamma masters of an essentially therapeutic, palliative consumerist culture. The secular university has also an intractable vested interest in the advocacies found fashionable since the 1960s: these, sadly, constitute the intellectual limit of many of the professoriate. Meanwhile, Christian liberal arts colleges have for the most part been backward in this regard. *O felix culpa*. That is as much as to say, these smaller schools have not been able or willing to hire the Ivy-league devotees of postmodern factions who have become tenured denizens of the would-be-Ivy private and publicly-funded schools of the second rank. Instead, most Christian liberal arts colleges have plodded along, out of step, teaching Chaucer, Shakespeare, Milton, and other "uninteresting" authors. Often, to be sure, they have done so in less than ideally informed and intellectually probative ways, but nevertheless with such earnest regularity that the English curricula of such institutions may now look to a habituate of the MLA rather like a fossilized remnant of a naïve former age—which it is likely to be, in fact, and blessedly so. In our present context, backwardness may prove to be a platform for future salvation.

A key decision for the future of English literature may thus rest not with those entrapped in the worldwide web of trendy advocacies and political correctness, but rather with those whom such powers have been pleased to deem foolish and irrelevant. The decision about what is worth teaching is not less vital for its province at the margins; in many respects, the smaller Christian liberal arts colleges that remain faithful to their mission may well become what monastic communities of learning were in the demise of the Roman empire: archival cultures, citadels for the light of learning in a dark and perhaps even barbarous time. Liminality with respect to present fashions may lead to centrality for future possibilities of intellectual seriousness.

Of course, the Christian liberal arts colleges, which to this point have had not only a more "old fashioned" English Literature curriculum but the proportionately larger following among undergraduate majors may well miss the opportunity through a failure of nerve. Some already have, out of apprehension of that shame to which American Christians are particularly vulnerable, namely the embarrassment of being thought unfashionable. But there are numerous institutions, some Catholic, some evangelical or reformed, which offer a Literature curriculum that provides a worthy *habitus*, a gathering of furniture for the Christian mind. The key decision for all such institutions now is how to strengthen what remains and add judiciously to it. For there are modern works of literature most worthy, and these must be carefully selected out of the general rubbish.

Another key decision pertains to the intellectual rigor with which such a curriculum should be taught. It is not enough for a healthy education that students should read and casually reflect on a work of superior literary merit. Christian liberal arts colleges, remembering that a training to read discerningly is the very foundation of their own religious cultures, should commit themselves afresh to teaching students to read for discernment. They should train for excellence in critical evaluation according to substantially objective principles, and test the principles even of alien interlocutors to see in what measure their insights might lend strength to their own practice. Above all, they should employ great literary texts in such a fashion as to give full weight to their concern for truth, and to clarify thereby, in the discussion of the various species of fiction, what is meant by both critical and moral realism.[16]

To do this work effectively in the twenty-first century, it is almost imperative that we recognize that the diminution of English-speaking national cultures has been to some considerable degree complemented by a rise in global literatures in English as well as by the availability of world literature in English translation. Reading comparatively is not only good global citizenship but also a species of Christian courtesy in which love of neighbor extends to the thoughtful consideration of the neighbor's best writers. One of the challenges here is to select for greatness in the international canon—for intellectual merit and consummate artistry as well as moral probity and clarity of cultural criticism such as may prove profitable to our own self-examination of cultural conscience.

At each such juncture we should recollect that Christian literary tradition has always made fruitful use of alien sources. It has managed this balancing of cosmopolitan outreach and coherent identity not through acquiescence to an alien *ethos* or idolatry of their idolatries but through appropriation of otherness selectively, especially to the degree that the insights prove revelatory of deep, universal truths. Thus Augustine, fully aware that the Greeks had, in the light of the Scriptures, gotten much wrong, nevertheless recommended importation of the best of their writing with an eye to the integration of their learning in a pursuit of Christian wisdom.

> If those who are called philosophers, especially the Platonists, have said things which are indeed true and are well accommodated to our faith, they should not be feared; rather, what they have said should be taken from them as from unjust possessors and converted to our use. Just as the Egyptians had not only idols and grave burdens which the people of Israel detested and avoided, so also they had vases and ornaments of gold and silver and clothing which the Israelites took with them secretly when they fled, as if to put them to a better use. They did not do this on their own authority but at God's commandment, while the Egyptians unwittingly supplied them with things which they themselves did not use well. In the same way all the teachings of the pagans contain not only simulated and superstitious imaginings and grave burdens of unnecessary labor, which each one of us leaving the society of pagans under the leadership of Christ ought to abominate and avoid, but also liberal disciplines more suited to the uses of truth, and some most useful precepts concerning morals.[17]

Augustine's "Egyptian gold" remains an appropriate intellectual principle, employed with discernment and charity, and without idolatry.

(Egyptian gold, it should be remembered from the Exodus account, can as easily yield up a golden calf as vessels for worship in the tabernacle.) But even as Augustine himself did not disdain to appropriate alien critical principles from the heretic Tyconius the Donatist in an ordered quest for Christian truth,[18] so we should, with critical eyes fixed firmly on the goal of our students' Christian intellectual formation, make selective use of the best literary and critical texts at our disposal. We do this when we grant to each text its distinctive voice, "hear it out," then consider what it says to us in our different circumstance. Only then should we attempt to appropriate what seems rational and ordinate for ongoing consideration of a particular issue.

This is to anticipate reflection on a final decision that confronts the discipline presently. The issue should be of great interest to Christian teachers of English Literature, but it often presents itself in such a way as to confound the generous intentions of those who would seek to incorporate an "interested" approach to method. It may be helpful if I develop this one point with an extended example.

Intertextuality and the Teaching of Literature

The term "text," as is well known, derives from the Latin *texo*, "to weave"; "to join or fit together"; "to intertwine," "interleave," "interlace," and thus "fabricate." A *textum* is thus "that which is woven; a web"; all that is text implies the bringing of diverse strands into a unified pattern, making meaning of elements that, without the patterning, would remain scattered, woolly and unfocused, unreferenced.

"Intertextuality," on this account, is simply an axiom of the presence of texts—or of textual tradition. In the weaving of human narrative, there are variations upon a cortex of central lines; the geometry (or syntax) of the original *textum* sets certain limitations upon the possibilities projected from the cortex, even as it encourages development and expansion of all that this cortex makes possible. When Jorge Luis Borges, in his provocative story, "The Gospel According to Mark," offers to reduce Penelope's web to its common denominators, in however draconian a fashion he reflects a confidence in the principles of interconnectedness and ultimate coherence the textual "metaphor" proclaims.

Throughout all recorded history, his narrator asserts, people "have always told and retold *two* stories—that of a lost ship which searches the Mediterranean seas for a dearly loved island, and that of a god who is crucified on Golgotha."[19] Well, this is too simple. Nevertheless, it is certainly indicative. In the romance, human aspiration is figured in the pilgrim epic-romance journey toward life in a promised land. In the bitter irony of the countering tragi-comedy, that aspiration is admonished with a hard saying: that the pathway to life lies through the Valley of the Shadow of Death. The two stories are not, I think, as Northrop Frye thinks, parallel epics.[20] They might be better understood as point counter-point, fundamentally related, meeting each other, recurrently, often at right angles.

Frye's tendency in his commentary to unweave the fabric so as to render parallel what had before existed in tension, though intertwined, is in consequence more reductive than Borges's observation. Yet Frye's view, in its own assumption of pre-existing pattern, is *less* reductive, fundamentally, than the notion of intertextuality which captivates many (recently) more fashionable post-structuralist theorists. Even in Barthes, a text "consists of multiple writings" issuing from widely diverse cultures and contexts, but the place where the weaving takes place is not in the text or "the author, as we have hitherto said it was, but the reader. . . . [T]he unity of a text is not in its origin; it is in its destination; but this destination can no longer be personal."[21]

The transience and instability of this fragile weave yields readily—among those who follow the Barthes model—to a further claim, namely that the various threads (narrative, poem, commentary, commentary-upon-commentary) hold equal status as pattern-generating elements. Here is the summary of George Steiner:

> The post-structuralists, the deconstructionist reminds us, say (justly) that there is no difference in *substance* between primary text and commentary, between the poem and the explication or critique. All propositions and enunciations, be they primary, secondary or tertiary (the commentary on the interpretation of interpretations, the criticism of criticism so familiar to our current Byzantine culture) are part of an encompassing

intertextuality. They are equivalent as *écriture.* It follows [from this way of thinking] . . . that a primary text and each and every text it gives rise to is no more or less than a *pre-text.* It happens to come before, temporally, by an accident of chronology. . . .

The poem or play, thus considered, is strictly anonymous. . . . The notion that we can grasp an author's intentionality is [on such an account] utterly naïve.[22]

In this view then, "intertextuality" is preeminently an *unweaving,* a deconstruction and—to use a Kierkegaardian idiom—"leveling," in which no hierarchies of value, or geometries of possibility or foundation, or even native syntax remain. The textual elements are completely *disassembled* so as to permit, it is argued, a "fabrication" which owes nothing to the order of their generation, or to any order of fact and value that origin may have expressed. "Intertextuality" in this usage is a function of the leveling and emptying-out of meaning, not a function of unfolding tracks of patterning in the weave, and hence can tell us nothing of the accretion and enrichment of meaning.

Now in the Christian tradition of literary theory, intertextuality is of the essence of textual significance. It begins in both the self-conscious and unself-conscious interlocution of biblical texts: higher truths are encoded in narrative, renewed in the Deuteronomic formula, echoed and meditated upon in the Psalms, reiterated and woven into the fabric of prophetic and apocalyptic narrative. At each stage there is an accumulated weight; the weave is both denser (in the sense that it is more resonant) and more "charged" with a surplus of meaning and possibility.

In the New Testament the cortex of this weaving is declared to be Christ, the *Logos,* and the whole force of the New Testament as interpretation of the Old is to "read" the pattern in the weave Christocentrically. For St. Paul, it is not only true that all texts in the tradition are rendered more intelligible by the *kerygma,* but that the *Logos* from the beginning firmly contextualizes the possible significance of all future writings. This is the point seized so ardently by Augustine, and which in his own literary theory becomes the characterization of "intertextuality" and even the "meaning" of human language itself (*OCD* 1.2.2). Meaning is not achieved by a *reductio* or leveling but by preservation of differences in an ongoing, self-correcting conversation in which understanding grows out of thoughtful comparison. The process is by instinct, in the radical sense "conservative," in its operation dialectical, and in its result affords the possibility of probative critical judgment precisely because the conservative and intersecting elements are not elided.

All such considerations pose a deeper question for practitioners in the guild of literary instruction who would wish to operate as thoughtful Christians. It might be phrased in something like this fashion: can we make use of our own grand narrative and the great conversation it has helped to engender more intelligently than perhaps has been recently the case? I think that the answer to this question must certainly be "yes, we can do this."

English Literature and the Other Disciplines

I have suggested that there has been a loss of prestige for English literature among the disciplines. One measure of that is surely in general academic reputation. Each in their own fashion, critics such as Matthew Arnold, Arthur Quiller-Couch, I. A. Richards, F. R. Leavis, C. S. Lewis, T. S. Eliot, Alan Tate, Cleanth Brooks, Lionel Trilling, Northrop Frye, R. S. Crane, and Wayne Booth have in their time been regarded as wisdom figures of a sort who, whether in a setting such as the Socratic Club at Oxford or the interdisciplinary colloquia under Robert Hutchins in Chicago, obtained the respect of philosophers, historians, and theologians. They were, moreover, read and critically engaged by these colleagues. More recently, the most luminous exemplars of the discipline have been figures of notoriety, their conferences written off as antics, and their work decreasingly granted the general attention even of humanists in other disciplines. The question here might be, "What could recapture the discipline from its own self-willed marginalization and move it back to the center of humanistic learning?" Another might be, "What is there now in common between English literary studies and other disciplines which could be developed in such a way as to make for greater intellectual neighborliness?"

My own thoughts on this point are tentative and insufficiently learned. Moreover, they are inevitably framed by my own intellectual history and that is the grain of salt with which they should be entertained, if at all, by the readers of this volume. Nevertheless, let me venture here my conviction that disciplinary isolation has been unfruitful, even crippling, for English Literature. Hypertrophy in the "omniversity" generally has tended to stifle conversation across the disciplines, but in graduate programs such narrowing has meant that very few new Ph.D.s have sufficient command of the curriculum to feel comfortable teaching even the basic "Beowulf to Virginia Woolf" survey (in places where such a survey is still taught). Moreover, whereas once Ph.D. programs typically required a reading knowledge of two modern European languages other than English, as well as of Latin or Greek and Anglo-Saxon, many new Ph.D.s have only a slight knowledge of perhaps one other modern language. Denied access to the golden treasuries of other literatures except in translation, and perhaps even disinterested in such a secondary effort, such monoglots have in their pursuit of multiculturalism imbibed a kind of intellectual xenophobia. As I have argued elsewhere, in condoning such a turning inward, we have not loved our neighbors as ourselves.[23]

I am inclined by experience to think that this sort of intellectual isolationism is less pronounced in the Christian liberal arts college than in the secular university, and that this is yet another reason students can generally hope for a better-rounded education in such places. It also suggests a departure for adding strength to strength in the Christian liberal arts college, in which even if theology is no longer, as in the medieval university, "queen of the sciences,"[24] it nevertheless provides a plenum of notional commonality amongst the humane disciplines in particular. Theology, Biblical Studies, Philosophy, English, and Comparative Literature are all text-based disciplines, each of which has arisen in some fashion in dialogue with a common Book. This fact of our intellectual history, when it is respected and kept alive through continuous exploration, cross-conversation, and rediscovery, is perhaps the single most enriching hope for the future of literary studies as a humane intellectual enterprise.

The rhetorical question of Tertullian that lingers at the base of all the reflections in this volume, repeated by Jerome and again by Alcuin in the eighth century, is still the great framer of other questions for literary study in a Christian context. "*Quid enim Hinieldus cum Christo?*"—"What has Ingeld to do with Christ?"—is metonymic for all questions about the integration of faith and learning in a Christian educational context. But if we would answer it, or its many analogues, in our own time, we might begin by reversing the proper names: "What has Christ to do with Ingeld?" Fortunately for Ingeld—as for Ovid and Catullus before him—the answer Christians have given since the Great Commission is "everything." Not only have Ingeld and Ovid been preserved to new life by Christians' love for the neighbor and for truth not their own; by their active engagement in intelligent conversation, the riches of Christian learning itself have been, increment by increment, increased. The biggest challenge for English Literature as a discipline today may be loss of all such capital—intellectual, artistic, and cultural capital. To the degree that we can agree on this point, the primary challenge for Christians in the discipline may well be to determine how to restore and activate that capital, and then judiciously to add to it so that a great investment by many generations is not squandered away.

Chapter 4 Notes

1. See, for example, *The Fiction of Jack Hodgins* (Toronto: ECW Press, 1989); "Encoding and the Reader's Text: Northrop Frye's *Great Code*," *University of Toronto Quarterly* 52 (1982/3): 137-143; "Real Presences: The Critical Project of George Steiner," *Religion and Literature* 22.1 (1990): 101-110.

2. See my "Biblical Scholarship and the Rise of Literary Criticism," in Rafey Habib, ed., *The Cambridge History of Literary Criticism*, vol. 6 (2011); also Stephen Prickett, *Words and the Word: Language, Poetics and Biblical Interpretation* (Cambridge: Cambridge University Press, 1986), 37-94; Nicholas Boyle, *Sacred and Secular Scriptures: A Catholic Approach to Literature* (Notre Dame, IN: University of Notre Dame Press, 2005), 3-57.

3. Prickett, *Words and the Word*, 63-65; David Lyle Jeffrey, *People of the Book: Christian Identity and Literary Culture* (Grand Rapids and Cambridge: Eerdmans, 1996), 308-315.

4. In this context, Theodore Dreiser's *Tragic America* (New York: Horace Liveright, 1931) remains invaluable primary reading.

5. Archibald MacLeish, "Ars Poetica," in *Literature: An Introduction to Poetry, Fiction, and Drama* 4th edition, ed. X. J. Kennedy (Glenview, IL: Scott Foresman, 1987), 674-675.

6. Ingeborg Hoesterey, ed., *Zeitgeist in Babel: The Postmodernist Controversy* (Bloomington, IN: Indiana University Press, 1991).

7. For Derrida, see J. Greisch, K. Neufeld, and C. Theobald, *De la Crise Contemporaine du Modernisme à la Crise des Herméneutiques* (Paris: ADD Publisher, 1973), 157; cf. Jonathan Culler, *On Deconstruction: Theory and Criticism after Structuralism* (Ithaca, NY: Cornell University Press, 1982). Culler has subsequently grown alarmed at the disarray in the discipline, and called for a return to formalist criticism as a remedy (MLA, *Profession*, 2003).

8. Terry Eagleton, *After Theory* (New York: Basic Books, 2003). An important critique of Eagleton's stance by Alan Jacobs may be found in *First Things* 214 (2011), 21-26.

9. John François Lyotard, *The Postmodern Condition: A Report on Knowledge*, trans. Geoff Bennington and Brian Massumi (Minneapolis: University of Minnesota Press, 1984).

10. Jeffrey, *People of the Book*, ch. 3-7.

11. Arnold, *God and the Bible* (London: Smith, Elder & Co., 1875), 7.

12. T. S. Eliot, "Religion and Literature," *Selected Prose*, ed. John Hayward (Hammondsworth: Penguin, 1953), 31-33.

13. C. S. Lewis, *They Asked for a Paper* (London: Geoffrey Bles, 1962), 48-49.

14. The national trend marks have been variously estimated as a drop between twelve and thirteen percent.

15. See, for example, A. Begley, "The I's have it: Duke's '*Moi*' Critics Expose Themselves," *Lingua Franca* 4.3 (1994): 54-59. This was among the first of many articles in the public sector to expose this now well-attested condition. See also Andrew Delbanco in *The Chronicle of Higher Education* (Sept. 5, 2008) and his lengthy review article, "The Decline and Fall of Literature," in the *New York Review of Books* 46.17 (Nov. 4, 1999); the latter of these is an important and devastating critique. Unfortunately, this chapter was written before a lively volume was published

which expresses its own distinctive concerns that "the Marsden settlement" is not as robustly and thoroughly Christian as believing historians should aspire to be: John Fea, Jay Green, and Eric Miller (eds), *Confessing History: Explorations of the Christian Faith and the Historian's Vocation* (Notre Dame, IN: University of Notre Dame Press, 2010).

16. For a fuller argument on this point, see David Lyle Jeffrey and Gregory Maillet, *Christianity and Literature: Philosophical Foundations and Critical Practice* (Carol Stream, IL: InterVarsity Press, 2011), esp. ch. 1 and 9.

17. D. W. Robertson, Jr., trans., *On Christian Doctrine* (New York: Macmillan / Library of Liberal Arts, 1958), 2.40.60; cf. 2.18.28.

18. Ibid., 3.35ff. For a discussion, see "Self-Examination and the Examination of Texts: Augustine's *Confessions* and *On Christian Doctrine*," in David Lyle Jeffrey, *Houses of the Interpreter: Reading Scripture, Reading Culture* (Waco, TX: Baylor University Press, 2003), 39-53.

19. E. R. Monegal and A. Reid, eds., *Borges: A Reader* (New York: E. P. Dutton, 1981), 310.

20. Northrop Frye, *The Secular Scripture: A Study of the Structure of Romance* (Cambridge, MA: Harvard University Press, 1976), 15.

21. Roland Barthes, *Image-Music-Text*, trans. Stephen Heath (New York: Hill and Wang, 1977), 147.

22. George Steiner, in *Real Presences* (Chicago: University of Chicago Press, 1989), trenchantly adds, "The deconstruction of the 'I' and of authorship separates the aesthetic from the ethical. Where is responsibility, where is responsible response to be located?" (101). His detailed critique of Barthes and Derrida (116-134) is lucid and helpful.

23. David Lyle Jeffrey, "Faith, Scholarship and Wisdom," *Current Issues in Catholic Higher Education* 24.2 (2005): 11-24.

24. See Al Wolters, "No Longer Queen: The Theological Disciplines and Their Sisters," *The Bible and the University*, eds. D. L. Jeffrey and C. S. Evans, vol. 8 of the Scripture and Hermeneutics Series (Milton Keynes, UK: Paternoster; Grand Rapids: Zondervan, 2007), 59-79.

EVANGELICALS, THE ACADEMY, AND THE DISCIPLINE OF HISTORY

Timothy Larsen

Unsurprisingly, the instinct of an historian is to approach a conversation about the integration of faith and learning in the discipline of history by first surveying the terrain historically. Therefore, this essay will begin with a narrative describing how we arrived at our present situation before moving on to reflections regarding the road ahead. The background context for this narrative is that for much of the twentieth century, the Christian faith was given rather short shrift in the discipline of history, especially when it came to modern history. There are a couple of reasons for this that need to be highlighted here.

One was the widespread assumption of the secularization thesis. Secularization theory assumed that an inevitable result of modernity was that religion became a decreasingly significant force in society.[1] In other words, to put it crudely, religion was dying off (at least on a public level) and was either already irrelevant to the course of history or soon would be. In a critique of this view, the philosopher Charles Taylor has spoken of a "stadial consciousness" in which it was generally assumed by many scholars that faith belonged to an earlier stage of human development to which it would be impossible to return.[2]

Moreover, secularization theory tended to skew even how history was treated before it was thought to have occurred. This is the case in my own area of specialization, Victorian Britain. For example, while twentieth-century scholars often conceded that religion was still alive and well in that period, they nevertheless focused their research on nineteenth-century doubters and freethinkers, seeing them as telling forerunners of the course of human history as these scholars imagined it is unfolding.[3]

The second factor was that Marxism became a prominent fashion in the philosophy of history during the decades after World War II. Marxist historians tended to reject the view that religious beliefs and motivations were significant forces in history and were apt to dismiss them as masks for, or distractions from, the real issues—namely, economic and class realities. One of the most influential books of modern British history, for instance, was E. P. Thompson's *The Making of the English Working Class*. Thompson was the son of missionaries who, by the 1940s, had become a committed Marxist. He dismissed the meaning of the Methodist revival in the lives of ordinary Britons as a "reflex of despair," that is, merely a pathetic manifestation of the bleakness of their situation regarding the real issues of class.[4] Eric Hobsbawm was another prominent figure in a whole group of leading British historians from that period who approached the discipline from a Marxist perspective. An additional manifestation of this tendency was that it became fashionable to argue that the abolition of the British slave trade was not the result of the Christian convictions energizing the actions of figures such as William Wilberforce but rather was simply the result of slave plantations (allegedly) becoming less economically profitable. Eugene D. Genovese was one of the most prominent Marxist historians in post-War America.

Both of those intellectual commitments have now been dethroned from their former places of strength. Many intellectuals were bewildered to discover the persistence and power of religious belief in the modern age. One of the leading champions of secularization theory in America had been Peter Berger, the author of an influential study, *The Sacred Canopy*. Berger made a public recantation in 1998: "In the course of my career as a sociologist of religion I made one big mistake . . . . The big mistake, which I shared with almost everyone who worked in this area in the 1950s and 60s, was to believe that modernity necessarily leads to a decline in religion."[5] While militant secularists might assume that religion is a pernicious force in modern history, even they usually no longer can convince themselves that it is not an authentic and powerful force. Likewise, the collapse of Communism has meant that subsequent generations of historians have, by and large, distanced themselves from Marxism even as an intellectual tool.

In this shifting context in which religion was again being perceived as a possibly important theme in modern history came the rise of "the new evangelical historiography."[6] This phrase refers to a cohort of evangelical historians that came to prominence in the 1980s. Its core was often identified as George Marsden, Mark Noll, and Nathan Hatch.[7] Non-Reformed fellow travelers included Grant Wacker, Edith Blumhofer, and (openly and vocally dissatisfied with the Calvinist ethos of the perceived core) Donald Dayton.[8] Beyond the United States, the late George Rawlyk was a leading figure in Canada, as was (and is) David Bebbington in Britain.

Significantly, the members of this cohort—although self-identifying as evangelical—carefully positioned themselves and their work inside the wider academy and the mainstream history guild. A rarity for evangelical scholars at that time, they had earned their Ph.D. degrees at prestigious research universities—Yale (Marsden), Vanderbilt (Noll), Harvard (Blumhofer and Wacker), Cambridge (Bebbington), and so on. Their research articles have been published in leading peer-review journals and their books with elite university presses. The trailblazer was Marsden's celebrated *Fundamentalism and American Culture* which appeared in 1980 from Oxford University Press.[9] Two years later came a collection of "essays in cultural history" edited by Hatch and Noll, also published by Oxford University Press. Others contributing to this volume—so that it came to feel like a kind of family outing—included Marsden, Wacker, and Harry S. Stout (a member of the network who has gone on to a distinguished career as a professor of history at Yale).[10] In 1994, Oxford University Press published the record of what might be seen as the great, international, English-speaking world, family reunion of evangelical historians, edited by Noll, Bebbington, and Rawlyk.[11] If the references to OUP are becoming monotonous, one could mix things up by recalling that Hatch's extremely influential *The Democratization of American Christianity* was published by Yale University Press, Wacker's well-received *Heaven Below* was by Harvard University Press, and so on.[12]

Beyond primarily chronicling this history, we need to transition to also offering a more evaluative assessment of ongoing trends, patterns, concerns, and opportunities. The context of this section is that many more evangelical historians who are in the trajectory of the cohort have emerged since the 1980s. A fair number of them were supervised by a member of the cohort. Marsden, in particular, has trained up an army of historians. My colleague here at Wheaton, Kathryn Long, for example, did her doctoral dissertation under Marsden's direction. (This research became an Oxford University Press book and won the American Society of Church History's Brewer Prize.)[13] During 2007-2009 I was privileged to be part of a four-person team of evangelical historians awarded a CCCU Initiative Program Grant. Steve Alter of Gordon College organized it; he would be an example of someone trained outside the network (his Ph.D. is from the University of Michigan, Ann Arbor—Alter has a couple of monographs with John Hopkins University Press), but the other two members of the team were both Marsden students: Thomas S. Kidd of Baylor University (who has monographs with both Yale University Press and Princeton University Press), and Sarah Miglio, a highly talented historian who recently completed her doctorate at Notre Dame. As for others trained outside the network, Bruce Hindmarsh at Regent College, Vancouver, who did an Oxford DPhil and publishes with Oxford University Press, is a first-rate historian, as are Doug Sweeney at Trinity Evangelical Divinity School, who did his Ph.D. at Vanderbilt and has published books with both Oxford University Press and Yale University Press; Thomas A. Howard, who teaches at Gordon College, did his Ph.D. at Virginia and has published with both Oxford and Cambridge University Presses; John Coffey, who is a professor of history at the University of Leicester, did his Ph.D. at Cambridge, and publishes with Cambridge University Press; and Sujit Sivasundaram, who teaches at Cambridge, where he did his Ph.D., and who also publishes with CUP.[14] These are meant merely as off-hand and haphazard examples of how the network is continuing and not necessarily as a survey of the most important evangelical historians of the subsequent generations. If speaking autobiographically may be forgiven, I did my BA thesis and MA work under Noll's mentoring and my Ph.D. under Bebbington's supervision. The assessment that follows, therefore, is my own, reflecting both my conscious desire to follow in the path mapped out by the Noll-Bebbington generation, and my own convictions, experiences, and situatedness, which differ from theirs in some ways.

When it comes to the integration of faith and learning, the new evangelical historiography has been attacked (from very different quarters) for failing to uphold adequately both components of that mixture. Let's first address the critique that they have sacrificed "faith"—the integrity of full, robust, and distinctively Christian convictions—in order to gain credibility and acceptance in the wider academy. Iain H. Murray of the *Banner of Truth*, for example, has expressed his uneasiness about this:

> My last comment is to point out that this book is part of the series of *Studies in Evangelical History and Thought* (with Editors David Bebbington, John Briggs, Timothy Larsen, Mark Noll, and Ian Randall). Most titles published in this series, as with Warner's title, seem to be work presented as doctoral theses in British universities. We can be thankful that the universities thus provide time and opportunity for men [sic] to do advanced study which few others can attempt. This also means that for a number of areas of research we are increasingly dependent on material coming from the contemporary academic world. Should that be at all disturbing when, as in this series, the authors are professed evangelicals? We think it should, and that because the British universities commonly impose a qualification that inevitably affects the work done: *The Bible is not to be treated as the Word of God*. So for a student to express value judgments based on Scripture is not acceptable procedure. . . . The effect of this qualification is to secularize church history and theology and to treat Christianity as another human discipline.[15]

A specific manner in which this concern is often framed is to object to the way in which the new evangelical historiography works within the confines of methodological naturalism. In other words, these historians refrain from making pronouncements that certain historical events outside the biblical record of salvation history are the direct result of divine action in some specific, heightened, identifiable sense from others. The alternative method is called "providential" historiography—history writing that does evoke divine motives and actions to explain or interpret particular historical events. A leading champion of this approach is Steven J. Keillor, who has argued that church historians can and should discern that particular acts in modern history were divine judgments for identifiable sins.[16] He contends that in an effort "to gain professional status and a hearing in the public square," the new evangelical historians have capitulated to restrictions that make their message less than what a fully Christian one ought to be.[17]

I myself write academic history using methodological naturalism. This is not, as is often said or at least implied, a mere pandering to the secular academy, a refusal to say all that I know or ought to know as a believer in order to gain outside recognition. Nor, on the other hand, is it because I am the kind of Christian who thinks that we can never have access to a divine perspective on contemporary events. (Keillor's book is framed around his disappointment that so many evangelicals refused to address the question of whether the 9/11 attacks were a divine judgment.) In contrast to a kind of at least soft cessationism that was often tacitly assumed by the Reformed core of the cohort in its formative phase, I am robustly charismatic. This means that I heartily believe that the divine meaning of contemporary events may be disclosed to us by prophetic words, visions, dreams, and the other ways that the Holy Spirit supernaturally imparts insights to human beings. What I object to, however, is the assumption that doing historical research generates such insights. This is to confuse the work of an academic historian with the ministry of the prophet. Events by themselves are too ambiguous—good things happen to bad people, bad things happen to faithful people—to identify definitively any such cause-and-effect chain by natural means. To declare that an earthquake is a divine judgment and not just a tragedy to be endured is to speak for God; and, more to the point, to declare "thus saith the Lord" without being inspired by the Holy Spirit is a foolish, dangerous, and indeed sinful, act. A major theme of both the Bible and the Christian tradition (not least Reformed thought) is that God's ways are often inscrutable.

It is true that there is a sense in which ordinary believers who are neither prophets nor the sons or daughters of prophets rightly make sense of history, especially their own personal history, by having a working confidence that they have discerned some divine meaning. It is extremely important, however, that historians do not pass off these general, Christian hunches for the results of their expertise as scholars. The only advantage that I have as an academic historian is a detailed grasp of the historical evidence regarding what exactly happened. This means that I can rule out certain misguided ideas. In wrestling with the legacy of Darwinism, for example, students have told me that Charles Darwin did not think the process of evolution applied to human beings and that he converted to Christ on his deathbed. These statements are simply not tenable as accounts of the evidence and so must be set aside. Beyond such corrections, however, there is no reason to assume that I have any specific insight to offer on what God was up to in a given situation because I am a trained historian. This expectation, however, is precisely what my students do assume. In other words, it is easy to have a transference occur in which my expertise on the historical evidence is mistaken for spiritual insight into God's actions. I think evangelical historians have a duty to dispel this self-aggrandizing, but groundless, expectation. Not to do so is potentially an abuse of power or position. Once again, even if my spiritual hunch is right, it does not arise from my expertise as a historian.

There is a tactical aspect to this as well, as the critics have suspected, but I think such strategic considerations are well nigh unavoidable as they are much more fundamental than merely the desire to gain acceptance by secular scholars. The truth is that providential perspectives are dependent on quite specific prior theological and ecclesial commitments. In other words, such history writing is a form of discourse that is limited to making applications for people who already think exactly like the author. Providential historians have said by way of rebuke that they want to be able to say in their books that the Great Awakening (the founding moment of evangelicalism) was a work of the Holy Spirit, and I should as well. As a charismatic, I tend to ask in reply about the founding moment of Pentecostalism, "And the Azusa Street Revival?" To which I generally get a polite, dissembling answer. In other words, as soon as one wants to address an audience one ring wider than or a half step adjacent to one's own particular ecclesial and theological identity, one needs to forgo writing on the basis of certain spiritual hunches that one has. Even Keillor did not want to write a book for only Republicans or Democrats and therefore he comments: "To analyze God's judgments as falling on both political parties is not to equate them or to measure their respective failings (which only God can do)."[18] It is precisely this parenthetical concession that only God can make certain calls that Keillor's book is supposed to be challenging, yet even he sees its utility and force up to a certain point. Therefore, a primary question is: what audience is the historian seeking to address? It can be appropriate, in my view, to write church history for a specific ecclesial audience which assumes providential perspectives. It would be wrong, however, to pretend that this historical work was "proving" that it particularly pleases the Almighty to bless the work of Baptists or whomever rather than merely taking such a stance for granted. Furthermore, as that example implies, mature reflection would be needed to avoid complacent connections where, for instance, the growth of one's own movement is always a sign of divine favor (when it could actually be a sign of capitulation to pernicious cultural trends). It is unfair to imagine that a desire to write for an audience that would include non-Christians should invariably be viewed pejoratively as selling out. Historically, one form of such writing the Christian tradition has called "apologetics" (a genre that requires plenty of respectful prudence), and there are other forms of faithfulness besides that one that could prompt a person to write for this wider readership.

Objecting from the opposite side, some non-evangelical historians have expressed their suspicions that the new evangelical historiography is so infused with faith that it has compromised "learning," that is, authentic, credible scholarship. In this view, evangelical historians are engaged in a kind of covert operation through which readers might unwittingly be duped by religious propaganda in disguise. In this critique, readers may think they are obtaining the objective results of the work of academic historians when actually these findings have been rigged by theological commitments. Bruce Kuklick, a professor of history at the University of Pennsylvania, went so far as to dismiss the very aspiration of the new evangelical historians to integrate faith and learning as "loony."[19] He later accused them of "bad faith"—a play on words by which he means that they are not really conforming to the standards of the wider academy, but only pretending to do so: "Christian historians really reject the position of critical history yet simultaneously argue as if it were true."[20] Likewise, John Kent, a professor at the University of Bristol, outed the existence of the cohort for unwary readers, citing the Noll-Bebbington-Rawlyk collection and Bebbington's *Evangelicalism in Modern Britain* as examples: "It is not unfair to call these books 'history in the service of the Faith,' which is what ecclesiastical history, Catholic as well as Protestant, has normally and openly been; one reads accordingly."[21] In other words, these historians are still creating scholarship governed by the old, providential framework; they are just not "openly" admitting this aspect of their work to readers but rather are trying to sneak it in without them noticing.

While I think these charges are unfair, they likely do reflect the fact that these critics are sensing that integration is really happening—that the faith of the new evangelical historians does inform their work. I think it is precisely because the members of the cohort and their heirs have been able to do this successfully without violating the scholarly conventions of the guild that their work is so annoying to suspicious observers such as Kent. How, then, does one's faith infuse and guide one's scholarship even when it is done within the boundaries of methodological naturalism? There is a whole range of ways, only some of which will be identified here. One is the choice of subject matter. Christian historians find certain life stories, events, and movements more interesting than their secular counterparts tend to do. A related matter is how a project is cropped—every historical study must set boundaries, but evangelical and secular historians tend to have different instincts about what they want to leave out of view. For example, Christabel Pankhurst, the leader of the Suffragettes, is an extraordinarily famous woman in Britain. To take one manifestation of this, the *Guardian*, a leading British newspaper, announced in 1999, "The Top 10 Women of the Millennium," that is, the most important women in *global* history (not just British) during the last *thousand* years. Pankhurst was named in this preeminent pantheon.[22] Nevertheless, I was stunned to discover that no academic historian (and only one non-academic historian—a journalist—and he rather incompetently not to mention unsympathetically) had ever done research into Pankhurst's influential ministry as a Christian preacher and writer, which she pursued after the right for women to vote was achieved. In contrast to previous scholars, I did not desire to crop my study of Pankhurst so as to cut off this part of her life.[23]

Secondly, while methodological naturalism does not allow for identifying specific divine interventions definitely, evangelical scholars can and do leave space for such explanations as part of the overall picture. I say "part" of the picture because there are generally second-order explanations as well. Exploring these is not the equivalent of denying a divine, first-order one, despite the fact that some of the faithful sometimes nervously imagine that this is so. (To observe that Billy Graham was charming and had a great sense of humor is not to deny that his ministry was effective because of a specific gifting and anointing of the Holy Spirit.) To take a biblical example, we are told: "Immediately, because Herod did not give praise to God, an angel of the Lord struck him down, and he was eaten by worms and died" (Acts 12:23 NIV). To say that he was "eaten by worms" is not to deny that there was also a divine action behind this event. Moreover, the academic historian could well have access to the coroner's report which identifies the worm infestation but, as a historian, does not have access to any angelic incident reports. Making space for the reality of the supernatural can change the tone of historical writing significantly. In particular, it means that, in contrast to some secular historians, evangelical scholars are not giving reductionist explanations which eliminate spiritual ones *a priori*. In my own field of nineteenth-century British religious history, it is quite common to read explanations of why people went to church that evacuate all spiritual meaning—assuming, for example, that church attendance was merely a way for them to gain social respectability. Again, it is not that such explanations are necessarily wrong as that they are incomplete: evangelical historians can write in a way that takes seriously the desire of some people to draw close to God in worship. As a charismatic, I often want to leave room for a story of healing to be interpreted as a miraculous act of God, perhaps even in answer to a specific prayer: I believe *both* that this is quite possible and that such an explanation should not be eliminated as a viable interpretation *and* that I generally do not have the evidence and tools as a historian to declare that this was the case definitely.

Another related aspect is an attitude of sympathy. This approach can change the tone of a piece of scholarship dramatically without making it uncritical or unscholarly. For example, for many secular historians, missionaries appear in their work only as cartoon villains. Evangelical scholars, by contrast, while not ignoring the gross failings of certain missionaries, might also write studies about other missionaries who ought not to be seen as figures of loathing or ridicule, but rather as human beings—patiently and resolutely making costly sacrifices—who defended the rights of indigenous peoples against the rapacious actions and policies of colonial governments and foreign companies.

There also are numerous ways in which specific, Christian theological commitments may inform the way that evangelical historians pursue their work even if many secular historians might have arrived at these commitments by other routes. For example, one historiographical trend since World War II has been "history from below," that is, not assuming that the subjects of history writing should be "great men"—kings, presidents, generals, and the like—but rather attending to ordinary people—peasant women, coalminers, domestic servants, and so on. While Marxist historians had their own reasons for being interested in social history, for Christians it can be grounded in a theological conviction that every human being is made in the image of God and therefore their lives have intrinsic value that makes them worthy of study. One could go on in this way—these musings on the difference that being a Christian can make for doing historical work are merely suggestive rather than exhaustive.

A historiographical trend in the wider academy that came after Marxism was postmodernism. Indeed, my experience has been that postmodern historians often turned out to be washed-up Marxist ones trying to remarket themselves. (As I mentioned him earlier, I should note that Eugene D. Genovese, on the other hand, discovered the

Catholic faith and moved in a more conservative direction.) One criticism made by postmodernists was that history writing had hitherto purported to be presenting "the facts" about the past when in actuality it was a form of fiction.[24] When the fashion for postmodern historiography was at its height, my tendency was to respond in a somewhat Socratic manner. I would first try to get my interlocutor to concede that this provocative claim was less devastating than they assumed. Is it not true that the best fiction is deeply and profoundly true? On the other hand, is there not also bad fiction that woefully misrepresents the human condition? If so, then we are still left with the fundamental distinction that history writing can be more or less truthful and so there is a need to evaluate it on the basis of this criterion. I would also point out that fiction comes in different genres and these genres have their own conventions. There are, for example, standard "rules" for writing detective fiction. One of these is that readers should have access to the same clues that the detective does so that they can try to reach the same conclusions independently. Obviously, an ingenious author might violate this rule and still write a satisfying book, but if done too often, the rule would break down and along with it the genre: there would be no more proper detective fiction being written, but rather, newer works would have slid into another category—thriller, crime, psychological study, adventure, morality tale, or whatever. My argument was therefore that even if one assumed for the purpose of argument that history writing was akin to fiction writing, it would still nevertheless be a particular genre of fiction, complete with its own set of rules. For historians, the conventions of their genre include, for instance, that one does not invent quotations and attribute them to historical figures, but rather one cites a source that allows other historians to track it down and check its accuracy. This also means that there are ways to discern between history writing that is better and worse, that is more or less satisfying. The real way that postmodern historiography was deflated, however, was through the publicity given to Holocaust deniers purporting to be historians. This jolted the guild into reaffirming its conviction that some things are known actually to have occurred and thus that history writing can recount real events and not just contestable, imaginative interpretations and perspectives.

Marsden has argued that because postmodernism has weakened the old, liberal hegemonic assumptions regarding scientific truth and reopened the door to scholarship arising from diverse ideological commitments, this ought to mean that explicitly Christian scholarship is once again acceptable in the wider academy.[25] As cogent as this argument is, I am not optimistic about its being implemented. It is certainly true that history writing is affected by the perspective of the author. One postmodern response to this insight has been to encourage everyone to declare their situatedness from the outset. A difficulty of this approach, however, is that, in practice, it is not a level playing field: some autobiographical details function to allow one's scholarship to be accepted with *less* critical scrutiny, while others are pounced upon to justify dismissing a scholar's work without even having to engage it—except with simply a knowing, "they would say that, wouldn't they?" This is obvious even if the realm of religion is set aside, and it leads scholars to highlight some parts of their identity and obscure others. Thus, whole shelves of books and articles have been written by scholars who have stated up front that they are writing, for instance, as a woman and a feminist, but who do not declare that they are also writing as a white, affluent, tenured professor at an Ivy League university and as a citizen of the world's only superpower. In short, my instinct is that declaring that one is writing as an evangelical does not mean that—having given full disclosure—one's perspective is going to be received on an equal footing with others. Quite to the contrary, it could well mean that critics do not feel they even have to bother to attempt to refute the evidence that you have spent years of your life carefully gathering and the insightful interpretations that you have painstakingly developed on the basis of it.

My own view is that the historian who tells the most compelling narrative wins. Our task in the years ahead should be to tell more compelling stories—more interesting, with evidence that has been more fully and effectively marshaled, with more convincing and illuminating analyses and interpretations. This does not mean that we pretend we have no situatedness and are just presenting an objective account of the past. It does mean, however, that it is a deeply Christian insight to observe that people make sense of their situation by understanding it in the context of a narrative. One way to see the discipline of history is as an ongoing effort to help people make sense of their lives by describing the narratives that they find themselves in or offering them alternative ones. The task ahead should not be primarily to complain about a bias against Christianity in the existing historiography, but rather for evangelical historians who have the vision and verve to rise up and tell better stories that reshape the conversation in a particular field in ways that are more faithful from a Christian perspective. More contentiously perhaps, my own view is that evangelical historians have tended to overdo narratives of declension. These have limited utility in the wider academy because they simply feed into a secular assumption that Christianity is defeated or in the process of breaking down and therefore can be ignored. (Some evangelical historians need to put the following verse in front of the computer screen where they do their writing: "Do not say, 'Why were the old days better than these?' For it is not wise to ask such questions." Ecclesiastes 7:10). My own experience is that secular scholars are very comfortable with grumpy, fearful, defeatist evangelical scholars documenting the rapid rate of the loss of all they value and rise of all they despise, but they are rattled and unsettled by witty, confident, urbane, evangelical scholars. Far from this being merely a tactic or form of capitulation, such a posture, at its best, can be an expression of faith—of confidence in the victory of God and the lordship of Christ. Who but Christians really believe that the story we inhabit ends as a comedy and not a tragedy?

One area in which this needs to be done also highlights part of the interdisciplinary way forward for evangelical historiography. A portion of evangelical historians needs to consider doing work in the field of the history of the disciplines. Many academic disciplines currently tell their own histories in anti-Christian ways that are eminently assailable. Emerging evangelical scholars in these other fields often find themselves living in narrative frameworks that are inherently hostile to an aspiration to integrate faith and learning. I, for example, have made a modest attempt to tell a better story about the history of the relationship between Christianity and science.[26] I learned many things from this experience, including that scientists (unlike historians) actually read their journals. I received e-mails from professors and graduate students at universities, colleges, and medical schools thanking me for the article. As many evangelical historians work at small institutions, they do not have the luxury, temptation, or doomed fate to stay in a silo conversation with only the other historians in their department. This kind of interdisciplinary work is therefore also a way that evangelical historians can be a service to their colleagues across campus. One of the informal mottos of the new evangelical historiography is that Christian scholarship is collaborative scholarship.[27] As a charismatic, this has particular resonance for me as it evokes the apostle Paul's teaching that we are all different members of one body who need each other. The volume you are reading now is a fine example of Christian, collaborative scholarship. One reason why the cohort made and continues to make such an impact was because it was greater than the sum of its parts. At a crucial, formative stage in their careers, those historians energized one another, served one another, opened doors for one another, challenged, instructed, and trained one another—reading and commenting on each other's work, convening conferences together, writing grants together, editing volumes together, and, indeed, even vacationing together. The future must include new professional friendship networks being forged by emerging evangelical historians who provide support and encouragement to each other.

In the long run, evangelical historians must move beyond the current base camp in the subdiscipline of religious history. The current phase, however, is a necessary one and, in my view, it is not over yet. In the same way that African American intellectuals for some time were generally preoccupied with issues of race and women intellectuals were at a certain stage largely focused on issues of gender, so the evangelical community has not gained a secure enough place in the wider academy yet and therefore, as advocates for our community, our intellectuals must attend to issues of religion. There must come a day, however, when some of the greatest evangelical historians specialize in other subfields, say, Latin American economic history or Chinese political history. Nevertheless, even when that day comes, it is unlikely that these scholars will have anything like the name recognition or profile of the likes of Marsden or Noll. If they do, it would probably not be because they are evangelical but rather because they happen to be among those rare historians who reach a general audience along the lines of figures such as David McCullough or Simon Schama.

More immediately, there is a need for evangelical historians to arise whose work is informed by a diverse range of theological and ecclesial commitments. It is not a critique but simply an observation to notice that the cohort has had a predominantly Reformed flavor. We need more leading evangelical historians who are reflectively working within other streams such as Methodist, Anabaptist, Lutheran, and Pentecostal, drawing on the theological resources of those traditions with depth and sophistication. These historians should not confine themselves to telling the story of their own people, but should also bring the perspective of their theological commitments to bear on other areas. (For example: might an evangelical Anabaptist historian bring different instincts to studying the French Revolution than an Anglican would?)

Finally, it should be recognized that the integration of faith and learning is an aspiration rather than a fixed template that can be inherited. Integration is hard, and we need to admit that sometimes we are not sure about the best way forward in a given area or in regard to a particular methodological issue. Each new generation and each new area of study requires original and painstaking wrestling with the question of what it means to be a faithful Christian doing scholarship with integrity in the context at hand. While I have tried to a certain extent to identify a good path for evangelical academic historians to follow, all of us must continue both to be willing to take new risks and to reevaluate regularly whether we have gone astray.

In summary, the future of evangelical historiography should be marked by both continuity and change. The continuity should include maintaining the pursuit of excellence in the wider academy; continuing to affirm that the confines of methodological naturalism can be appropriate and helpful in certain contexts; steadfastly allowing one's faith to infuse and guide one's scholarship in numerous ways such as choosing subject matter, making cropping-choices, leaving room for supernatural realities, and bringing sympathetic approaches to bear; and nurturing the practices of collaborative scholarship and supportive networking. The change should include the emergence of more diverse ecclesial perspectives; the entry of more leading evangelical historians into other subfields beside religious history; a more substantial interdisciplinary effort, perhaps with a particular focus on the history of the disciplines; and a greater tendency to resist the temptation to pursue only declension narratives. Most of all, let's try to provide more interpretively powerful and compelling narratives in which people can situate themselves, their experience, and their task ahead in liberating, strengthening, and faithful ways.

Chapter 5 Notes

1. For my own interdisciplinary critique of secularization theory, see Timothy Larsen, "Dechristendomization as an Alternative to Secularization: Theology, History, and Sociology in Conversation," *Pro Ecclesia* 15.3 (Summer 2006): 320-337.

2. Charles Taylor, *A Secular Age* (Cambridge: Harvard University Press, 2007), 289.

3. While its heyday was earlier, such scholarship continued right to the end of the century: see, for example, A. N. Wilson, *God's Funeral* (New York: W. W. Norton, 1999). For my attempt to expose this tendency and offer a correction to it, see Timothy Larsen, *Crisis of Doubt: Honest Faith in Nineteenth-Century England* (Oxford: Oxford University Press, 2006).

4. E. P. Thompson, *The Making of the English Working Class* (London: Victor Gollancz, 1965 [originally 1963]), 177.

5. Peter L. Berger, "Protestantism and the Quest for Certainty," *Christian Century*, 115.23 (1998): 782; see also Peter L. Berger, "The Desecularization of the World: A Global Overview," in *The Desecularization of the World: Resurgent Religion and World Politics*, ed. Peter L. Berger (Grand Rapids, MI: Eerdmans, 1999), 1-18.

6. Leonard I. Sweet, "Wise as Serpents, Innocent as Doves: The New Evangelical Historiography," *Journal of the American Academy of Religion* 56.3 (Fall 1988): 397-416.

7. Maxie B. Burch, *The Evangelical Historians: The Historiography of George Marsden, Nathan Hatch, and Mark Noll* (Lanham, MD.: University Press of America), 1996.

8. For an example of Dayton's concerns, see Donald W. Dayton, "'The Search for the Historical Evangelicalism': George Marsden's History of Fuller Seminary as a Case Study," *Christian Scholar's Review* 23.1 (1993): 12-33. For a reflection on some of these tensions, see Douglas Sweeney, "The Essential Evangelical Dialectic: The Historiography of the Early Neo-Evangelical Movement and the Observer-Participant Dilemma," *Church History* 60.1 (1991): 70-84.

9. George M. Marsden, *Fundamentalism and American Culture: The Shaping of Twentieth-Century Evangelicalism, 1870-1925* (New York: Oxford University Press, 1980).

10. Nathan O. Hatch and Mark A. Noll, eds., *The Bible in America: Essays in Cultural History* (New York: Oxford University Press, 1982).

11. Mark A. Noll, David W. Bebbington, and George A. Rawlyk, eds., *Evangelicalism: Comparative Studies of Popular Protestantism in North America, the British Isles, and Beyond, 1700-1990* (New York: Oxford University Press, 1994). Alternatively, one might see it as the great meeting of the heads of the families of the evangelical "mafia" of historians. The mafia tag was common at the time. Burch's concluding chapter is even entitled, "An Evangelical Mafia?" (Burch, *Evangelical Historians*, 116-122). As that little joke is rather stale by now, however, I have tried here to introduce the nomenclature of "the cohort" instead.

12. Nathan O. Hatch, *The Democratization of American Christianity* (New Haven: Yale University Press, 1989); Grant Wacker, *Heaven Below: Early Pentecostals and American Culture* (Cambridge: Harvard University Press, 2001).

13. Kathryn Teresa Long, *The Revival of 1857-58: Interpreting an American Religious Awakening* (New York: Oxford University Press, 1998).

14. Coffey's name is a suitable prompt for mentioning an important edited volume on religious history after the decline of secularization and Marxist theories

which includes chapters by Bebbington and Noll as well as younger scholars: Alister Chapman, John Coffey, and Brad S. Gregory, eds., *Seeing Things Their Way: Intellectual History and the Return of Religion* (Notre Dame, IN: Notre Dame University Press, 2009).

15. Iain H. Murray, "Reinventing Evangelicalism," *Banner of Truth*, 15 February 2008, www.banneroftruth.org.

16. Steven J. Keillor, *God's Judgments: Interpreting History and the Christian Faith* (Downers Grove: IVP Academic, 2007).

17. Ibid., 15.

18. Ibid., 18.

19. He was interviewed for an article in the *Chronicle of Higher Education*; see also Bruce Kuklick and D. G. Hart, eds., *Religious Advocacy and American History* (Grand Rapids, MI: Eerdmans, 1997), 16. Marsden anticipated this reaction in the very title of a seminal study: George M. Marsden, *The Outrageous Idea of Christian Scholarship* (New York: Oxford University Press, 1997).

20. Bruce Kuklick, "On Critical History," in Kuklick and Hart, *Religious Advocacy*, 59.

21. John Kent, *Victorian Studies* 41.1 (Autumn 1997): 109.

22. "The top 10 . . .", *Guardian*, 25 January 1999, *www.guardian.co.uk*.

23. Timothy Larsen, *Christabel Pankhurst: Fundamentalism and Feminism in Coalition* (Woodbridge, UK: Boydell Press, 2002).

24. For a collection exploring this conversation, see Brian Fay, Philip Pomper, and Richard T. Vann, eds., *History and Theory: Contemporary Readings* (Oxford: Blackwell, 1998).

25. For example, see George M. Marsden, *The Soul of the American University: From Protestant Establishment to Established Nonbelief* (New York: Oxford University Press, 1994), 430-431.

26. Timothy Larsen, "'War Is Over, If You Want It': Beyond the Conflict between Faith and Science," *Perspectives on Science and Christian Faith* 60.3 (September 2008): 147-155.

27. I inherited this from Mark Noll whom I believe would attribute it to another member of the cohort—possibly George Rawlyk.

FIVE UNEASY QUESTIONS

Or, Will Success Spoil Christian Psychologists?[1]

Mary Stewart Van Leeuwen and Jade Avelis

Who am I? How, in my view, is the Christian faith related to psychology? How has this relationship changed, for better or worse, over the past few decades? As we enter the second decade of the twenty-first century, are Christian psychologists handling their dual identities better than in the past? What future directions should Christian psychologists consider? These are five "uneasy questions"—in the sense of both "troubling" and "complex"—that Christians within the field of psychology must encounter and answer in time.

They are sources of unease because they imply deeper questions about the definitions of "psychology" and "Christianity," and whether "relationship" is even the best term to connect them. Moreover, the diversity of psychology as an academic and applied discipline, and of Christianity as a religious tradition, is bound to make any person's answers seem parochial at best and arrogant at worst. Nevertheless, in the spirit of fools rushing in where angels fear to tread (cf. Prov. 12:23; 13:16), I offer the following remarks.

Some Autobiographical Remarks

"All research is autobiographical." That was what cultural anthropologist Paul Bohannon dared to tell students during my graduate school days in the early 1970s, when positivism was the ruling epistemology because most social scientists had yet to read Thomas Kuhn's *The Structure of Scientific Revolutions*[2] or Michael Polanyi's earlier challenge to the received view of science.[3] But Bohannon's assertion made intuitive sense to women students and students of color, who had noticed—though lacking the resources to challenge it at the time—that both academic and clinical branches of psychology consistently supported the white, male *status quo*.[4] Later, as a more serious Christian, I was to note that both also presumed a godless universe based solely on the laws of physics and/or evolutionary biology, or alternatively on the tenets of individualistic humanism.[5] Psychology's view of human beings thus vacillated "between reductionism and self-deification,"[6] and its philosophy of science remained, for the most part, unreflectively positivistic.

But in the 1970s and 80s, feminists, critical theorists, and a host of postmodern philosophers of science demonstrated the degree to which scientific data are theory-laden and theories are underdetermined by facts.[7] It is now widely accepted that individual and group "standpoint" concerns necessarily affect the conduct of science, that all seeing is "seeing as," and that, *contra* positivism, there can be no such thing as "immaculate perception" or a "view from nowhere" in scientific—much less social scientific—work.[8] Nor, on the applied level, can there ever be completely non-directive therapy.[9]

These accumulating, postmodern philosophical challenges ring true to me for reasons of personal history and theological conviction. In my personal history, I am a Canadian with an American doctorate, married to an American with a Canadian doctorate. My in-laws were immigrants who spent most of World War II in the Dutch underground, helping to smuggle Jews to safety. My doctoral training in cross-cultural psychology (a field definitely in its infancy in the 1970s) was motivated by two years of high school teaching in Africa prior to graduate school. Such horizon-expanding experiences, along with the more routine one of being a woman in a man's world, increased my respect for perspectives other than the ones I had been trained to accept.

Theologically I am a Calvinist who believes in both pervasive depravity and common grace. The first of these doctrines holds that no human function or institution—Christian or otherwise—is free from the distortions of sin. Although it is true that unbelievers fail to acknowledge the sovereignty of God, this does not render believing Christians flawless (intellectually or ethically), but rather simply forgiven sinners through God's special grace. Common grace, by contrast, asserts that God's cultural mandate to "fill the earth and subdue it" (Gen. 1:26-28) is given to human beings in general, not to Christians alone. Calvinist historian James Bratt explains that common grace

> reconcile[s] the doctrine of total depravity with the presence of good among the unconverted, at the same time reaffirming God's sovereignty by making that good fruit of divine grace rather than human effort. . . . it encourage[s] the redeemed to respect the good remaining in the world and to strive to augment it. It [makes] many elements of human culture—institutions such as the law and the community, artistic and technical ability, academic disciplines, and scientific methods—not just the products but *means* of grace, instruments by which God restrain[s] sin and enable[s] men (*sic*) to try to develop creation as [God] had originally intended. Finally, it legitimate[s] a certain amount of cooperation between the redeemed and unbelievers on the grounds that to some extent they share a sense of the good and therefore a common purpose.[10]

So here is a paradox which continues to inform my life: On the one hand, I confess that Christians, through the converting work of the Holy Spirit and the witness of Scripture, have "inside information" lacking to others about the ultimate origin, structure, and purpose of human life; on the other hand, the cultural mandate and God's sustaining, common grace are not limited to believers, and pervasive depravity is not limited to unbelievers. That is why philosopher and theologian Abraham Kuyper could wryly observe, with regard to both intellectual and ethical matters, that "the world often does better than expected and the church worse."[11] Truth is thus a gift of God, whomever its human mediators happen to be. The perpetual challenge, of course, is to recognize it when we see it: to separate wheat from chaff in the work of believers and unbelievers alike.

The Unity of Faith and Learning in Psychology

I must confess up front that language about "the integration of faith and learning" is something of a red flag for me. To explain why, I need to summarize my convictions about the use of Scripture in scholarship.

In the redemptive-historical interpretive tradition of the Reformed churches, Scripture is a cumulative, God-directed narrative. Its successive acts (creation, fall, redemption, and future hope) comprise a cosmic drama in which all persons, whether consciously or not, are players. This means, first, that Scripture cannot be used atomistically. We cannot settle confessional, intellectual, or social conflicts simply by trading proof-texts, but must consider all issues in light of the entire redemptive-historical line of Scripture and with due regard to the area(s) of creation involved. Moreover, because Christians continue to travel this redemptive-historical path toward the new heaven and the new earth, they must always be ready to look at Scripture afresh—to clean their interpretive lenses, as it were, from the sin and finitude of their historical location. In this task, while Scripture as special revelation remains the ultimate authority, we are aided by tradition, reason, and experience—all sources (however imperfect) of God's general revelation. This implies, by extension, that understanding the relationship between Christian faith and any given discipline is an ongoing process which no one can claim to have fixed in amber for all time.

But seeing Scripture as a redemptive-historical drama implies something else, too: that all persons are "characters in search of an author," that is, fundamentally *worshipping* beings who, if not committed to the one true God, will inevitably end up revering some substitute within God's creation—material goods, social status, political power, personal pleasure, or even art and scholarship. On this account, the scholarly and professional lives of psychologists are not on a separate level from their religious convictions. If we are at heart worshipping beings, then the target of our worship will set a direction—consciously or unconsciously—for every other activity in our lives. Hence we cannot separate the conduct of psychology from our faith life (then somehow decide to integrate the two), because living and learning are constantly filtered through a prior faith-allegiance, be it to naturalism, theism, Marxism, nihilism, or any other worldview in the marketplace of ideas.[12] *All* persons, in Nicholas Wolterstorff's words, "reason within the bounds of religion."[13] That is why this section's title refers to the *unity* (not the integration) of faith and learning in psychology. It is also why Abraham Kuyper, on whose thought this position draws, refused over a century ago to accept the putative fact/value distinction of positivism. Something of a postmodern epistemologist before his time, Kuyper was convinced that *all* knowledge is worldview-based—indeed, that all of life is religious.[14]

In the previous section, I emphasized that valid theorizing in psychology is neither limited to Christians nor guaranteed by the traditional methods of social science. Nor, obviously, can a complete understanding of human behavior be gained from Scripture alone. Nevertheless, the Bible, while not a psychology textbook in the usual sense, provides us with certain background assumptions or "control beliefs"[15] by which Christians can both shape and judge psychological theories. Over against the reductionistic or self-deifying tendencies of contemporary psychology (as well as the deism of some of psychology's philosophical precursors), the Bible describes the universe as God's creation, constantly sustained by God's involved, providential care. It tells us that human beings are both "dust of the earth" and "made in the image of God." Intended to be God's accountable stewards on earth, we have bungled the job badly through our determination to be independent of God and need to know how to get straightened out. Conversion and sanctification are crucial to this process, yet neither guarantees earthly utopia: humans continue to live "between D-Day and V-Day"[16]—between Christ's resurrection (and accompanying gift of the Holy Spirit) and the final consummation when all things will be made new.

Stanton Jones[17] has shown how Christians can translate the contours of biblical drama into control beliefs for crafting, adjudicating, and testing psychological theories, without degenerating into a naïve biblicism or forcing inappropriate standards for truth based on positivist assumptions onto Scripture. If this drama is a trustworthy account of reality, it suggests that intrinsic (as opposed to instrumentally motivated) religiosity should correlate positively with indices of mental health, which has been demonstrated consistently across the literature.[18] It suggests that marriages which are committed, mutually respectful, and nonrigid with regard to gender will, over the long haul, be better for the health of children, adults, and society than the plurality of alternatives endorsed by left-wing and right-wing forces of political correctness.[19] It suggests that the presumption of limited human agency and moral accountability in both individuals and groups is a better starting point for therapy than either the mechanistic amorality of pure behaviorism or the expressive individualism of humanistic psychology.[20] It suggests that altruism is not always neatly reducible to the mechanisms of instrumental rationality, but that religious commitment in particular and worldviews in general are factors to be reckoned with by theorists trying to account for self-sacrificing behavior in persons.

In these and many other ways, biblical control beliefs are profoundly relevant for psychological theory, research, and practice. They constitute, as it were, the framework of the disciplinary house we are trying to build.[21] We must use available materials and our intelligence to add the siding, the floors, the wiring, and so on. As accountable stewards made in God's image, we have considerable freedom in doing this; moreover, there is nothing wrong with specialization of theory or method, provided neither becomes reductionistic. To pursue the analogy, some people can concentrate on the floor, others on the roof, others on the wiring, and so on. But to have a house that will endure, we must be working within the God-ordained limits of the framework. With regard to many issues in psychology, the Bible provides such a framework. Due to our creaturely limitations and sinful inclinations, we can probably never understand that framework with completely disinterested, ahistoric accuracy. But that does not except us from the responsibility to keep trying.

The Best of Times or the Worst of Times?

Is it harder to be a Christian psychologist now, compared to twenty-odd years ago? The answer depends on one's definition of professional success. On the applied level, it is not exaggeration to say that business is booming for Christian therapists, as indicated by the number of M.A., Ph.D., and Psy.D. programs mounted by Christian institutions of higher learning in the past three decades. Therapy, once seen by many Christians as a tool of the devil, or at best a covert admission of spiritual failure on the part of its users, is now a respectable activity to engage in. Ministers who once regarded therapists as intruders in their pastoral-counseling territory now cooperate in referring parishioners to them; some pastors even acquire professional counseling qualifications themselves.

From one point of view, this represents an admirable rejection of the nature-grace dualism which has plagued Christians in general, and American evangelicals in particular, since the time of the fundamentalist-modernist debate in the early decades of the twentieth century.[22] But from another point of view, the rush of evangelicals to the therapist's office may simply represent an historically separatist and collectivist subculture belatedly adopting the wider societal values of instrumental and expressive individualism.[23] Sociologist Robert Wuthnow, in his review of Mark Noll's book *The Scandal of the Evangelical Mind*, comments that

> American evangelicalism is the quintessential adaptation to a society dominated by the marketplace and consumerism. It is such a late-twentieth-century phenomenon that most evangelicals would hardly recognize themselves in Jonathan Edwards or George Whitefield. To be sure, evangelicals are generally devout, church-going Christians who take the Bible seriously and try to live in obedience to their Lord. But study after study shows that they seldom understand the Bible very well, know little about theology, buy heavily into the therapeutic culture of feel-goodism, and are caught up in a cycle of overspending like everyone else. In my view, this is the real scandal of American evangelicalism.[24]

It would be a dubious measure of success if the full appointment books of Christian therapists represent little more than a willingness to peddle cheap grace and unqualified individual fulfillment, in the tradition of much of the profession at large. That this may indeed be a problem is suggested by the example of rising divorce rates among Christians, and the impunity with which pastors and parachurch leaders in particular seem to discard their spouses. On this matter, much of church discipline is in a shambles, with "forgiveness," "emotional support," and "restoration to ministry" too often being the operative principles, regardless of the economic and psychological fallout visited on vulnerable children and ex-spouses.[25] As a non-therapist, I have little sense—anecdotal or systematic—of the extent to which Christian therapists cooperate in supporting this no-fault/no-responsibility view of divorce. But it is a question we would do well to ponder, even as we press our respective churches to develop an ethic which is neither legalistically punitive nor unconditionally accepting of divorce.

The situation for Christians in academic psychology is likewise ambivalent. On the one hand, the eclipse of positivism by a post-empiricist philosophy of science means that truth is no longer reduced to what is empirically or analytically demonstrable, with everything else (e.g., revelation, literary, and artistic productions) considered so much subjective "non-sense" in terms of truth-value. If all research is equally autobiographical, then the discipline's gatekeepers are no more justified in rejecting well-crafted theories based on a Christian worldview than ones coming from a feminist, socialist, psychobiological, or any other standpoint. This epistemological shift helps account for the sustained interest in Division 36 (Psychology of Religion) within the American Psychological Association since its official establishment in 1976.[26] Another indication of this change in the perception of religion in the psychological academy is the appearance of Jones' landmark article in *American Psychologist* outlining a constructive relationship for religion with psychology. [27] Since that publication, religion has continued to grow in importance in the discipline of psychology, shown by the publication of *Handbook of the Psychology of Religion and Spirituality*.[28] I suspect that none of these would have occurred even a quarter of a century earlier.

On the other hand, theorizing from a post-empiricist standpoint risks degenerating into epistemological relativism, on the assumption that everything which passes for knowledge is socially—or even individually—constructed.[29] This can lead to the indiscriminate debunking of both science and religion in their roles as partial and intertwined, yet valid, routes to truth. Alternately, both may be reduced to the status of ideological tool for those (e.g., clerics, technocrats, capitalists) bent on rationalizing their power in society. On this account, the only valid standpoint—epistemological or ethical—resides in those who are oppressed by class, color, gender, sexual orientation, or other victim status. Although it is a theologically dubious conclusion, victim status is assumed to confer, almost automatically, the epistemological advantage of "double vision" on its holders, since they have had to develop survival-based knowledge both about their own group and the hegemonic groups who have marginalized them.[30]

If either of these extreme scenarios became psychology's orthodoxy, it would not be propitious either for the discipline or for Christians within it. Epistemological relativism leads in the end to a self-stultifying failure of nerve in research and theorizing. A standpoint epistemology which privileges only the most oppressed encourages ever more group fragmentation as people rush to join the "victimization sweepstakes" in order to privilege their own limited take on reality. Psychology as a discipline needs to accept the humbling lessons of postmodern epistemology without degenerating into skepticism and/or splintered interest group enclaves which see no need for—or possibility of—communicating with each other or acknowledging any common goals.

In sum, lay Christians have adopted a more positive attitude toward psychology, and Christians in the discipline are now less marginalized in the wake of postmodern philosophical shifts. But the specter of epistemological relativism and the proliferation of standpoint theories, combined with the growing individualism of rank and file Christians, represent ongoing challenges.

Meeting in the Middle

What progress, if any, have Christian psychologists made in thinking about and practicing their dual identities? Setting aside for the moment my Calvinist discomfort with the language of dualism, I respond to this question with qualified optimism.

Through the 1980s, Christians were rather too sharply divided between those who defended a more traditional, pre-Kuhnian view of science for psychology[31] and those who, to varying degrees, embraced the emerging insights of postmodern philosophy of science.[32] The former were more or less committed (at least in principle) to the objectivity of the scientific method based on Popperian falsificationism[33] and to methodological determinism as a theoretical model, while at the same time rejecting both anthropological and epistemological reductionism. According to this view—labeled "perspectivalism" by Evans[34]—scientific and religious routes to truth operate on different levels, roughly equivalent to the distinction between general and special revelation, and while both are valid, they must not be mixed together. The latter, whom Evans[35] labeled "humanizers" or "Christianizers" of science, had absorbed lessons about the rule-governed nature of human action[36] and the power of paradigms,[37] and were concerned to show the extent to which metaphysical commitments influence all stages of scientific work—not just the contexts of theory and application, but everything in between, from the labeling of concepts, to choice of operational measures, to interpretation of data.

But now it is probably fair to say that both sides have moved toward a middle ground. Rather than assuming either that scientific theories can emerge—at least in principle—automatically from data ("naïve realism") or that theories are so paradigm-bound that they bear no relation to data at all ("radical anti-realism"), both sides appear to have embraced some form of "critical realism": the view that "although reality does not force one and only one structure on our perceptions, there are limits to the degree to which our preexisting conceptions can impose a structure on reality."[38]

This, in my view, is a reasonable compromise, which pays implicit respect both to the doctrine of creation and the doctrine of sin. On the one hand, it would have been strange indeed (not to mention unfair) if God had issued a cultural mandate to human beings to "subdue the earth" and to "till and look after the garden" (Gen. 2:15) without giving them the perceptual and cognitive capacities to make at least halting progress toward that end. Indeed, it would suggest that humans were not corporately made in God's image at all, but each stuck on a solipsistic little island, incapable of discerning a common reality or communicating meaningfully with each other about it. Since, confessionally speaking, this is not the case, some concession to a realist epistemology is in order. On the other hand, humans are finite and sinful creatures. We are historically embodied and physically limited by our species-life, so we can neither aspire to a "view from nowhere" nor completely erase the filters of self-deception from our scholarly lives. Paradigms can both help and hinder valid scientific theorizing, but either way, they are unavoidable. These doctrines, aided by insights from philosophy of science (not to mention research in perception and cognition), support some form of critical realism as the preferred stance of Christian psychologists.

Honesty should lead many of us to admit we have been trained as psychologists in an anti-theoretical, anti-philosophical tradition. We are therefore indebted to colleagues in other disciplines for some of the progress of the past four decades. Thus Browning[39] and Roberts[40] have used the resources of theology and philosophy respectively to examine the degree to which competing worldviews inform models of personhood and therapy, and another philosopher, Stephen Evans,[41] has done a helpful job of showing how empirical, hermeneutical, and value-critical approaches in psychology are necessarily intertwined. But psychologists are catching up in theoretical and philosophical sophistication, as evidenced by Propst's text on psychotherapy within a religious framework[42] and Jones' detailed, philosophy-sensitive monograph[43] calling for an explicit and constructive relationship between psychology and religion. The Paloutzian and Park text referenced earlier also attests to this broadening relationship, although much is left to be researched.[44]

Possible Directions for the Future

Evans defines Christian psychology as "psychology which is done to further the kingdom of God, carried out by citizens of that kingdom whose character and convictions reflect their citizenship, and whose work as psychologists is informed and illuminated by Christian character, convictions, and understanding."[45] He goes on to point out that such a psychology need not be totally unique: to the extent that God's norms for created life and God's cultural mandate are intended for everyone, we should expect to find pockets of common ground with honest intellectual seekers whose worldviews may be other than Christian.

I would go even further: non-Christian psychologists who have pushed naturalistic or humanistic paradigms far enough to become disenchanted with them may sound a prophetic note for reform even before Christians do. One example is William Doherty's volume on the need for therapists to recover and support virtues such as commitment, justice, truthfulness, and community in their clients, and to implement the virtues of caring, courage, and prudence in their own practices.[46] Another example is Frank Pittman's work on the distortions of cultural masculinity and the need to help men rebuild lives of committed engagement with wives and children.[47] Richardson and Zeddies have also identified the problems inherent in the rampant individualism at the heart of most modern psychotherapy.[48]

Christian therapists, at least in theory, are well placed to add their voices to such critical conversations, but few have done so in a way which could engage a wider readership. One exception is M. Gay Hubbard's volume on counseling women, which judiciously appropriates the best insights of feminist theory and therapy within an implicit framework of creation theology and biblical justice ethics.[49] I have yet to see a similar work on the challenges of doing therapy in cross-cultural settings, but such a volume is long overdue, especially in a world where non-Caucasian Christians are rapidly becoming the majority, yet where 11 o'clock on Sunday morning remains among the most segregated hours in America.

In the academic realm, Christians need to demonstrate intellectual competence while at the same time acquiring enough theological and philosophical sophistication to generate genuinely creative theory and research based on a biblical worldview. The lack of such creativity in the past was partly due to rigid, positivistic hegemony in the discipline, partly due to residual anti-intellectualism in some Christian circles, and partly due to sheer lack of resources. Clearly, the first of these obstacles has been substantially overcome, and the flourishing of Christian undergraduate and graduate schools suggests that the second problem may also be dissipating. As to the problem of resources, of course there is never enough funding for everything that needs to be done, but we can be grateful for foundation initiatives which have provided summer programs in Christian thought for gifted undergraduates, funding for Christian doctoral students attending top-ranking universities, and support for faculty summer seminars and post-doctoral research projects done within an orthodox Christian framework. In years to come, the ripple effect of such initiatives in both Christian and secular institutions will hopefully be considerable.

The general tone of my reflections has been one of cautious optimism, for the cultural and disciplinary *Zeitgeists* are, on the whole, more open to theistic points of view than has been the case for a very long time. Whether Christian psychologists as a group will be more spoiled or energized by these opportunities has yet to be seen.

Chapter 6 Notes

1. A special thanks to the editors of the *Journal of Psychology and Christianity* for their permission to use portions of an article by Mary Stewart Van Leeuwen that originally ran in their journal (15:2, 1996, pp. 150-160) as the basis for this chapter.

2. Thomas S. Kuhn, *The Structure of Scientific Revolutions* (Chicago: University of Chicago Press, 1970).

3. Michael Polanyi, *Personal Knowledge: Towards a Post-Critical Philosophy* (Chicago: University of Chicago Press, 1962).

4. Nancy Boyd-Franklin, *Black Families in Therapy* (New York: Guilford, 1989); Carolyn Wood Sherif, "Bias in Psychology," *Feminism and Methodology,* ed. Sandra Harding (1987); N. Weisstein, "Psychology Constructs That Female, of the Fantasy Life of the Male Psychologist," *Roles Women Play: Readings Towards Women's Liberation,* ed. Michele Hoffnung Garskof (1971).

5. Don S. Browning, *Religious Thought and Modern Psychologies: A Critical Conversation in the Theology of Culture* (Philadelphia: Fortress Press, 1987); Robert C. Roberts, *Taking the Word to Heart: Self and Others in an Age of Therapies* (Grand Rapids, MI: Eerdmans, 1993); B. D. Slife and M. Whoolery, "Are Psychology's Main Methods Biased Against the Worldview of Many Religious People?" *Journal of Psychology and Theology* 34.3 (2006); Mary Stewart Van Leeuwen, *The Sorcerer's Apprentice: A Christian Looks at the Changing Face of Psychology* (Downers Grove, IL: InterVarsity, 1982); Mary Stewart Van Leeuwen, *The Person in Psychology: A Contemporary Christian Appraisal* (Grand Rapids, MI: Eerdmans, 1985); Mary Stewart Van Leeuwen, *Gender and Grace: Love, Work and Parenting in a Changing World* (Downers Grove, IL: InterVarsity, 1990); Paul C. Vitz, *Psychology as Religion: The Cult of Self-Worship* (Grand Rapids, MI: Eerdmans, 1994).

6. C. Stephen Evans, *Wisdom and Humanness in Psychology: Prospects for a Christian Approach* (Grand Rapids, MI: Baker, 1989).

7. For example, David Bloor, *Knowledge and Social Inquiry* (London: Routledge & Kegan Paul, 1976); Mary B. Hesse, *Revolutions and Reconstructions in the Philosophy of Science* (Bloomington: Indiana University Press, 1980); Larry Laudan, *Science and Values* (Berkeley: University of California Press, 1984).

8. K. Gergen, "The Social Constructionist Movement in Modern Psychology," *American Psychologist* 40 (1985); S. L. Jones, "A Constructive Relationship for Religion with the Science and Profession of Psychology: Perhaps the Boldest Model Yet," *American Psychologist* 49 (1994); Michael J. Mahoney, *Scientist as Subject* (Cambridge: Ballinger, 1976); Thomas Nagel, *The View from Nowhere* (New York: Oxford University Press, 1989); Richard Rorty, *Philosophy and the Mirror of Nature* (Princeton: Princeton University Press, 1979); R. L. Sorenson, "How to Anticipate Predictions about Integration's Future Trends," *Journal of Psychology and Theology* 32 (2004).

9. A. E. Bergin, "Values and Religious Issues in Psychotherapy and Mental Health," *American Psychologist* 46 (1991); William J. Doherty, *Soul Searching: Why Psychotherapy Must Promote Moral Responsibility* (New York: Basic Books, 1995); J. W. Jones, "Training Supervisors to Integrate Psychology and Christianity," *Journal of Psychology and Christianity* 26 (2007).

10. James Bratt, *Dutch Calvinism in Modern America: A History of a Conservative Subculture* (Grand Rapids, MI: Eerdmans, 1984).

11. G. C. Berkhouwer, *Man: The Image of God* (Grand Rapids, MI: Eerdmans, 1962), 186.

12. R. K. Bufford, "Philosophical Foundations for Clinical Supervision Within a Christian Worldview," *Journal of Psychology and Christianity* 26.4 (2007); James W. Sire, *The Universe Next Door: A Basic World View Catalogue* (Downers Grove, IL: InterVarsity, 1988); Brian J. Walsh and J. Richard Middleton, *The Transforming Vision: Shaping a Christian World View* (Downers Grove, IL: InterVarsity, 1984); Albert M. Wolters, *Creation Regained: Biblical Basics for a Reformational Worldview* (Grand Rapids, MI: Eerdmans, 1985).

13. Nicholas Wolterstorff, *Until Justice and Peace Embrace* (Grand Rapids, MI: Eerdmans, 1983).

14. Bratt, *Dutch Calvinism*; Bufford, "Philosophical Foundations"; Wolterstorff, *Until Justice and Peace Embrace*.

15. Wolterstorff, *Until Justice and Peace Embrace*.

16. Oscar Cullmann, *Salvation History* (London: SCM, 1967).

17. Jones, "A Constructive Relationship," 184-99.

18. A. E. Bergin, K. S. Masters, and P. S. Richard, "Religiousness and Mental Health Reconsidered: A Study of an Intrinsically Religious Sample," *Journal of Consulting Psychology* 34 (1987); C. H. Hackney and G. S. Sanders, "Religiosity and Mental Health: A Meta-Analysis of Recent Studies," *Journal for the Scientific Study of Religion* 42 (2003); Dale A. Matthews, David B. Larson, and C. P. Barry, *The Faith Factor: An Annotated Bibliography of Clinical Research on Spiritual Subjects* (Arlington, VA: National Institute for Healthcare Research, 1993).

19. G. Kaufman, "Do Gender Role Attitudes Matter?: Family Formation and Dissolution among Traditional and Egalitarian Men and Women," *Journal of Family Issues* 21.1 (2000); Frank Pittman, *Private Lies: Infidelity and the Betrayal of Intimacy* (New York: Norton, 1989); Frank Pittman, *Man Enough: Fathers, Sons, and the Search for Masculinity* (New York: Putnam, 1993); Judith S. Wallerstein and Sandra Blakeslee, *Second Chances: Men, Women and Children a Decade after Divorce* (New York: Ticknor & Fields, 1989).

20. Larry Crabb and Dan B. Allender, *Encouragement: The Key to Caring* (Grand Rapids, MI: Zondervan, 1984); Doherty, *Soul Searching*; Slife and Whoolery, "Psychology's Main Methods."

21. Van Leeuwen, *Gender and Grace*, 30.

22. Marsden, *American Culture*; Mark Noll, *The Scandal of the Evangelical Mind* (Grand Rapids, MI: Eerdmans, 1994).

23. Robert N. Bellah, et. al., *Habits of the Heart: Individualism and Commitment in American Life* (Berkeley: University of California Press, 1985); Frank C. Richardson and Timothy J. Zeddies, "Individualism and Modern Psychotherapy," *Critical Issues in Psychotherapy*, eds. Brent D. Slife, Richard N. Willams, and Sally H. Barlow (Thousand Oaks, CA: Sage Publications, 2001); Philip Rieff, *The Triumph of the Therapeutic* (New York: Harper & Row, 1966); Michael A. Wallach and Lise Wallach, *Psychology's Sanction for Selfishness: The Error of Egoism in Theory and Therapy* (San Francisco: Freeman, 1983).

24. R. Wuthnow, "Review of Nark Noll's *The Scandal of the Evangelical Mind*," *First Things* 51 (1995): 41.

25. Elizabeth Marquardt, "No Good Divorce," *Christian Century* 123.3 (2006); R. E. Hughes and J. H. Armstrong, "Why Adulterous Pastors Should Not be Restored,"

Christianity Today 39.4 (1995); C. S. Streeter, "Whatever Happened to His Wife?" *Christianity Today* 39.4 (1995).

26. M. E. Reuder, "A History of Division 36 (Psychology of Religion)," in *Unification Through Division: Histories of the Divisions of the American Psychological Association*, 4th ed. Donald A. Dewsbury (Washington, DC: American Psychological Association, 1999).

27. Jones, "A Constructive Relationship," 184-99.

28. Raymond F. Paloutzian and Crystal L. Park, eds., *Handbook of the Psychology of Religion and Spirituality* (New York: The Guilford Press, 2005).

29. Gergen, "Social Constructionist Movement," 266-75.

30. Raewyn Connell, *Gender and Power: Society, the Person, and Sexual Politics* (Stanford, CA: Stanford University Press, 1987); Paulo Freire, *The Politics of Education* (South Hadley: Bergin and Garvey, 1985); Sandra Harding, *Whose Science/Whose Knowledge? Thinking from Women's Lives* (Ithaca, NY: Cornell University Press, 1991).

31. J. D. Foster, "North American Psychology Revisited," *Christian Scholars Review* 23 (1983); Malcolm Jeeves, *Psychology and Christianity: The View Both Ways* (Downers Grove, IL: InterVarsity, 1976); Donald M. MacKay, *The Clockwork Image: A Christian Perspective on Science* (London: InterVarsity, 1974); Donald M. MacKay, *Human Science and Human Values* (London: Hodder & Stoughton, 1979); Donald M. MacKay, *Brains, Machines, and Persons* (Grand Rapids, MI: Eerdmans, 1980); David G. Myers, *The Human Puzzle: Psychological Research and Christian Belief* (San Francisco: Harper & Row, 1978).

32. For example, C. Stephen Evans, *Preserving the Person: A Look at the Human Sciences* (Downers Grove, IL: InterVarsity Press, 1977); B. H. Hodges, "Perception, Relativity, and Knowing and Doing the Truth," *Psychology and the Christian Faith*, ed. S. L. Jones (Grand Rapids, MI: Baker, 1986).; Van Leeuwen, *The Sorcerer's Apprentice*.; Mary Stewart Van Leeuwen, "Response to a Faithful Apprentice's Response," *Christian Scholars Review* 23 (1983); Van Leeuwen, *The Person in Psychology*; Mary Stewart Van Leeuwen, "Psychology's Two Cultures: A Christian Analysis," *Christian Scholars Review* 27 (1988).

33. Karl Raimund Popper, *The Logic of Scientific Discovery* (New York: Basic Books, 1959).

34. Evans, *Preserving the Person*.

35. Ibid.

36. Peter Winch, *The Idea of a Social Science* (New York: Humanities Press, 1958).

37. Kuhn, *The Structure of Scientific Revolutions*.

38. Jones, "A Constructive Relationship," 187.

39. Browning, *Religious Thought and Modern Psychologies*.

40. Roberts, *Taking the Word to Heart*.

41. Evans, *Wisdom and Humanness*.

42. L. Rebecca Propst, *Psychotherapy in a Religious Framework: Spirituality in the Emotional Healing Process* (New York: Human Sciences Press, 1988).

43. Jones, "A Constructive Relationship," 184-99.

44. Paloutzian and Park, *Religion and Spirituality*.

45. Evans, *Wisdom and Humanness*, 132.

46. Doherty, *Soul Searching*.

47. Pittman, *Private Lies*; Pittman, *Man Enough*.

48. Richardson and Zeddies, "Individualism and Modern Psychotherapy."

49. M. Gay Hubbard, *Women: The Misunderstood Majority* (Waco: Word, 1992).

CHRISTIANITY, SCIENCE, AND THE HISTORY OF SCIENCE

Some Thoughts on the Integration of Faith and Learning

Edward B. Davis

Athens and Jerusalem: Introducing the Problem

Few areas of inquiry are more broadly interdisciplinary than efforts to relate science and religion. Christians have been engaged in lively conversations about this for a long time. Almost a thousand years before the founding of the first universities, the Carthaginian father Tertullian famously asked, "What indeed has Athens to do with Jerusalem? What concord is there between the Academy and the Church?"[1] Admittedly, Tertullian was not very interested in having a conversation, but his general hostility toward Greek philosophy, including what we now call science, was not widely shared. Several patristic writers saw both the Bible and Greek natural philosophy as valid sources of knowledge, and many saw the value of being well educated in pagan learning. As the great French scholar Henri-Irénée Marrou observed, "Christianity is an intellectual religion and cannot exist in a context of barbarism."[2]

At that point in time, there was no such thing as "science" in the modern sense: there was no independent enterprise devoted to the study of narrowly defined aspects of nature by carefully trained specialists. There were quite literally no "scientists" at all—that word was not used until 1833, when it was coined during a scientific meeting as a convenient term to refer collectively to those assembled there, practitioners of individual disciplines, such as mathematics, chemistry, and other sciences, that had already begun to separate unto themselves. The scholar who invented the word, William Whewell, noted "the want of any name by which we can designate the students of the knowledge of the material world collectively," and so he suggested that, "by analogy with [the word] *artist*, they might form *scientist*. . . ."[3] For more than two millennia, from the time of Aristotle in the fourth century BC down to the early nineteenth century, the closest equivalents to our words "science" and "scientist" were "natural philosophy" and "philosopher." This is not a trivial point. Those older terms carry with them clear overtones of the connections between and among areas of learning that are less clearly seen now.

Nevertheless, many important connections remain, especially when the topic is science and religion. For almost thirty-five years, I have been attending events devoted to various aspects of science and religion, and at many of those events the range of academic disciplines represented has been much wider than those represented at events devoted to most other subjects. One can get a sense of this, vicariously, by typing "science and religion" into the catalog of a college or university library, or by browsing the contents of several issues of some of the journals devoted to science and religion. Note the primary disciplines from which the authors come, and my point will almost certainly be made.

The integrative task is especially important for those of us who teach at Christian colleges, where we serve as mentors for other Christians who need to answer their own personal questions about science and faith.[4] Ideally, this will be done in a way that shows students multiple options and encourages students to explore more than one of them *actively, on their own*. The process of faith formation is intensely personal, and students often entertain doubts about the specific content of their faith. The great chemist Robert Boyle (1627-1691) understood this very well. Consider the following aphorism, which he wrote when he was twenty years old—the same age as most college students today: "He whose Faith never Doubted, may justly doubt of his Faith." Immediately before this, he had written, "The Dialect of Faith runs much upon the First Person[;] or True Faith speakes always in the First Person."[5] I bring a similar attitude to my teaching, especially in courses about Christianity and science. These are deep waters filled with complex issues, and I want to give students the kind of assistance they need to see their way through the muddle. As Oliver Wendell Holmes is reported to have said, "I would not give a fig for the simplicity on this side of complexity, but I would give my life for the simplicity on the other side of complexity."[6] What I aim to achieve is not indoctrination in any sense, but the creation of a supportive environment in which students are helped to draw their own conclusions and to evaluate the assumptions that accompany their faith, in order to help them take ownership of a faith that is genuinely their own.

Perhaps surprisingly, the doubts Boyle was referring to had nothing to do with science. He had not yet launched his career as a laboratory scientist, and as far as we know he had not yet given science a passing thought. However, he was very widely read in Latin, French, Italian, and English literature; his dearest friend and elder sister was trapped in a dreadful marriage; the family castle had been ruined in the Civil War; he had lived on the Continent for several years in the home of a man whose family had fled religious persecution; and he was subject to fits of depression. In short, Boyle had doubts because he lived a deeply thoughtful Christian life at a troubled time, with science adding only a further element, even if it was an element that kept him engaged in theological reflection for the rest of his life.

I don't think Boyle's experience was fundamentally different from our own. We still need to formulate our own understanding of the Christian faith, and doubts will still arise from many different quarters. For Christian education, this means that an interdisciplinary approach is much more likely to be effective at cultivating a lifelong engagement with matters of faith and learning. Christian educators already know this, and Christian colleges have general education requirements partly for this reason. But the sciences might not always be seen as having a crucial role in general education, especially not a role that is on par with courses in theology, history, philosophy, Bible, or literature. To some extent, this probably reflects the gap between the scientific and human-istic cultures that C. P. Snow brought into prominence more than fifty years ago.[7] It's hard for most people to see any humanity in an atomic weight or a differential equation, and hard to see any science in the Gospel of John or the disintegration of the Roman Empire.

Nevertheless, the sciences raise fundamental questions of mean-ing and value: what does it mean to be human, in light of genetics and neuroscience? What do we mean when we confess God as our Creator, in light of evolution and the Big Bang? What indeed are we to make of science itself, as an activity carried out by sinful and fallible human beings who are still created in God's image? These are inescap-ably interdisciplinary questions, involving the sciences but coming from the humanities, and they are among the most important questions we can ask. They are the kinds of questions that many of our students are asking and all of our students should be introduced to—whether or not the sciences are the principal focus of their academic studies. It takes interdisciplinary courses, whatever they are called and wherever they are housed in the curriculum, to do that most effectively.

The Conflict View of Science and Religion: The Main Problem Today

The fundamental problem is not simply that people in the modern West often find religion irrelevant to science, and vice versa; if that were the main sentiment, it would not be nearly as difficult to promote an interdisciplinary conversation. The situation is far more serious. Many scientists today, including a number of highly vocal eminent scientists, hold the view that Christianity and science have for two millennia been engaged in open and inevitable conflict, with science winning the war for cultural and epistemic territory. This attitude ultimately derives from the European Enlightenment prejudice against religion. We find an extreme form in post-revolutionary France, where the philosopher Auguste Comte, who invented the word "positivism," constructed a "Religion of Humanity" supposedly founded on science. In his view, knowledge progresses from an initial "theological" stage consisting of fanciful beliefs about the world, through a metaphysical stage involv-ing abstractions, and finally to a "scientific" stage of genuine "positive" knowledge.[8] Having vanquished traditional religion, science now puts on its mantle: science provides a value-laden creation myth, reveals our true human nature, proclaims the promise of material and cultural salvation, gives us every good and perfect gift, offers eschatological hope, and functions as the final arbiter of truth. When some of the most well-known scientific authors of our time do this, they are in effect creating a religion of science.[9]

Until recently, a weaker form of the conflict view was actually much more common and more influential. This one found its most famous expression in the United States in the decades following the Civil War, a time when science was coming to be seen as the engine of progress and universities were rapidly expanding and exerting their cultural authority independently of clerical connections. In 1874, chemist John William Draper of what is now called New York University published his *History of the Conflict between Religion and Science*, and in 1896, the first president of Cornell, historian Andrew Dickson White, published a massive two-volume work he had been working on for almost thirty years, *A History of the Warfare of Science with Theology in Christendom*. Although Draper's book was rather sharply focused on Roman Catholicism as the number-one enemy of progress—the doctrine of papal infallibility had just recently been proclaimed at the First Vatican Council in 1870—the overarching scheme he advanced was much more general and identical to that found today in many works that are not specifically anti-Catholic. As he put it in the preface, "The history of Science is not a mere record of isolated discoveries; it is a narrative of the conflict of two contending powers, the expansive force of the human intellect on one side, and the compression arising from traditionary faith and human interests on the other."[10] One can almost hear the orchestra rising to a crescendo, while Christianity exits quietly through a side door.

White's book advances a similar overall outlook. Contrary to the new atheists of our day, White believed that the Christian *religion* is still important for moral reasons; nevertheless, traditional Christian *theology* must be swept aside to allow the endless progress of scientific knowledge. In his view, theology has never had a productive conversation with science; it has never inspired scientific activity or influenced a valid scientific idea; it has done nothing but hold back the progress of science. White wrote the famous preface to his book while he was the American ambassador to czarist Russia, based in St. Petersburg on the banks of the River Neva, which freezes over completely in the winter. Every spring, the peasants would go out on the river just as the ice was starting to melt, chopping away at the barrier to prevent dangerous flooding with consequent damage and the spreading of disease. White introduced readers to his narrative with this memorable image, in which the rising river represented science and the ice represented traditional Christian beliefs:

> My work in this book is like that of the Russian *mujik* on the Neva. I simply try to aid in letting the light of historical truth into that decaying mass of outworn thought which attaches the modern world to mediaeval conceptions of Christianity, and which still lingers among us—a most serious barrier to religion and morals, and a menace to the whole normal evolution of society.[11]

White regarded the czars as barbaric and the character of the Russian people as having been tainted by the autocratic milieu. His book painted a similar picture of the history of science and religion, in which "vaunted scientific autonomy was achieved through the exceptional agency of great men striving against deeply pernicious character traits instilled by theological training," as it has recently been so aptly described.[12]

The late Stephen Jay Gould understood better than most modern scholars precisely what White was really trying to accomplish—not to advance a generic warfare of religion versus science, "but rather to save religion from its own internal enemies," especially "dogmatic theology"—a pejorative term for traditional Christian beliefs used by both White and Gould. In their view, science will always be in conflict with Christian theology, but not with religious attitudes and sentiments per se. A peaceful co-existence is possible, provided that religion abandons any factual claims that go beyond the moral realm. Thus, Gould proposed his famous "NOMA" model, according to which science and religion are two "Non-Overlapping Magisteria" that do not fight over the same epistemic territory, but only because theology has ceded so much to science.[13]

The books by Draper and White are widely influential today, perhaps partly because the false picture they paint is central to the apologetics of contemporary unbelief.[14] It is not hard to understand why advocates of the stronger form of the conflict model would embrace them. Ironically, many other thinkers in the contemporary religion/science dialogue, including many Christian theologians, also accept the basic attitude of Draper and White—without realizing it. They typically deny that science and religion are engaged in an ongoing, inevitable conflict, yet they actually agree with the main thrust of White's book: traditional theology has proven utterly unable to engage science in fruitful conversation, and therefore we must now fully reformulate our understanding of Christianity in order fully to embrace modern science.[15]

For example, let us consider a leading modern scientist-theologian, the late Arthur Peacocke. When Peacocke spoke of God as "the transcendent, yet immanent, Creator," he did not really mean the transcendent Creator in anything like the traditional sense, especially not the omnipotent maker of heaven and earth who literally became flesh in the person of Jesus Christ. Peacocke believed that Joseph was Jesus' true father, thus removing the paradox of the Incarnation—the central mystery of the Christian story—by essentially affirming Jesus' full humanity and denying his divinity. His view that God never acts "supernaturally" contradicts several of Jesus' miracles, such as the turning of water into wine or the raising of Lazarus. Above all, Peacocke denied that Jesus rose bodily from the grave, and he tried mightily to distance the gospel narratives of the empty tomb, which he could not bring himself to believe, from the post-crucifixion appearances of Jesus, which seemed to have for him a kind of reality that is yet not quite reality.[16]

Other theologians have similar views. I am immediately reminded of the testimony given by Roman Catholic theologian John Haught at the *Kitzmiller vs Dover* trial, when he was cross-examined by the lead counsel for the defense, Richard Thompson, who is also a Catholic. Toward the end of the exchange, Thompson reached under the podium, brought out a copy of the Catholic catechism, and used it to formulate questions for Haught about the Virgin Birth and the Resurrection. In responding, Haught declined to affirm anything like a traditional understanding of either doctrine. For example, if there had been a video camera in the upper room when Christ appeared to his disciples after the crucifixion, it would not have captured his image, because (apparently) it lacked faith.[17] Even though he has written eloquently in denial of the conflict thesis, it is hard to avoid the impression that Haught essentially agrees with White and Gould: theology must give way to allow the onward march of science.[18] A frank assessment of the overall situation comes from one of the most radical of contemporary theologians, David Ray Griffin, who says that "modern liberal theologies have achieved a reconciliation of science with *theology* at the expense of its religious content."[19] In my opinion, this is not a route we want to encourage our students to take.

The Relevance of the History of Science for the Modern Situation

The academic discipline I represent, the history of science, has taken the lead in debunking the conflict view of Draper and White.[20] Both the forest (their overall attitude) and many of the trees (specific examples of "conflict" they relate) are decayed. The forest fails entirely to convey the great richness and complexity of the real historical story of science and religion. By imposing on everything a single, ill-chosen conceptual box of perpetual and inevitable conflict, so many other events and ideas that do not fit into that box are left unmentioned, leaving readers with the profoundly erroneous impression that the conflict thesis has been demonstrated. As for the trees, let us simply consider White, who planted so many of them. Although he was a highly respected historian who served as the first president of the American Historical Association, his book is inexcusably sloppy. In many cases, he relied far too heavily on poorly researched secondary sources, failing to consult the original sources himself. Consequently, he reports numerous false "facts" and cites authors who never said what he "quotes" them as saying. Colin Russell, a former president of the British Society for the History of Science, was really a bit too kind when he observed that White's "prominent apparatus of prolific footnotes may create a misleading impression of meticulous scholarship."[21]

In addition to chopping down that forest, historians of science have also helped undermine the common image of science as purely objective knowledge and faith as purely subjective belief—a conception closely related to the conflict view. We now know that scientific knowledge is determined not simply by observations and experiments, but by the outcome of debates about how to *interpret* observations and experiments. These debates are influenced by a variety of factors—philosophical, religious, sociological, political, and personal. It is now possible as never before to see both science and religion as containing deeply held, rationally structured beliefs, some of them not directly testable.

What does this mean for curriculum design and delivery at Christian colleges and universities? First, students in all areas—but especially those who major in technical disciplines—should become acquainted with the conflict view and the "demythologizing" of it by contemporary historians. A more accurate view is not the polar opposite, however—everything has not always been harmonious, and it is not always harmonious now. There have been some genuine conflicts involving science and theology, and later I will address an ongoing source of conflict about origins. Nevertheless, a more accurate picture is significantly friendlier to people of faith than either form of the conflict view, and in any case our students ought to be taught the best current scholarship as part of the process of helping them to construct their own faith. Anything less does them a disservice. At the risk of being accused of partisanship, let me add that this particular task will probably be done most effectively by a historian of science, or at least by a general historian or someone else (perhaps a philosopher or a theologian) with some formal academic training in the history of science. Some scientists at Christian colleges have acquired a good working knowledge of some aspects of the history of science and religion, but to rely only on scientists to teach such courses is probably not the best long-term solution for all but the smallest of institutions.

I will put it as bluntly as I can: if this particular topic is thought to be really important—if this conversation is thought to be highly relevant to educated Christians in our time—then Christian colleges should be looking for highly qualified faculty to teach a full range of courses related to the humanistic aspects of science and to take institutional leadership over that part of the curriculum where such courses are housed. Such courses at Messiah College meet a general education requirement called "Science, Technology, and the World," which supplements another requirement for a course in laboratory science. Faculty currently teaching in this area represent psychology, the natural sciences, engineering, and philosophy, in addition to the history of science. At many Christian colleges, however, there is no comparable curricular home; there might be an isolated course somewhere, or there might be a senior seminar for science majors which is not open to other students (we have such seminars at Messiah, but we also have general education courses).[22] Thus, we have a classic case of the "chicken-and-egg" problem: without first having a curricular home for humanistic courses about science, institutions see no need to hire faculty with the strongest qualifications for teaching such courses. Even in the best economic times, it may always be easier to justify hiring one more laboratory scientist, or one more sociologist, or one more philosopher or biblical scholar, than to justify hiring someone whose specialty does not fall squarely within one of the academic majors taught at that institution. To the best of my knowledge, no Christian college presently offers a major focusing on the humanistic study of science, technology, or medicine. I am not advocating for change along those lines; I am simply advocating for the importance of intentionally hiring faculty with such training.

Although some scientists can acquire the knowledge and skills necessary to teach certain courses that are *about* science, rather than *in* one of the sciences, the very large pedagogical differences between those two types of courses must be understood and appreciated. To teach students about humanistic aspects of science, with the crucial component that students personally engage the issues, requires a certain pedagogy. Lectures alone cannot suffice and laboratory instruction is usually irrelevant. Significant amounts of reading, writing, and discussion of texts are essential—just as they are essential in other humanities courses. Scientists can learn to cross this bridge, but scholars in the humanities are already on the other shore. It may be wise for a scientist to teach this topic alongside a humanities professor, at least for a few years if not indefinitely. Both faculty members could potentially learn much from one another, not only in terms of course content but also pedagogically.

There is a further advantage of team teaching. It can be helpful for students to see, among the faculty, examples of those who hold different views on how to relate science to faith. This can be difficult or impossible to achieve at most Bible colleges and some seminaries and colleges, where adherence to a particular view of the Bible and/or a very narrow interpretive framework would work against genuine diversity in the integrative task. Students who are not exposed to this kind of diversity, whether by a single instructor or by a team, may be quick to identify integration with one particular way of doing it, and just as quick to abandon the whole enterprise when, later on, a seemingly insurmountable obstacle appears to lie along the one path that has been shown to them in a favorable light.

To round out this section highlighting the history of science, let me refer readers to the appendix, which contains a sample writing assignment. This is intended to prepare students for a lengthy discussion of a classic text that can be very effective in helping them think about the Bible in relation to science: the *Letter to the Grand Duchess Christina*, written in 1615 by Galileo Galilei. Precisely because the issue of concern to Galileo—the motion of the earth—no longer concerns us today, students are better able to evaluate his views with impartiality, taking what is helpful and applying it to other issues that do concern them. Regardless of what we think of the answers Galileo gave, he asked several of the right questions: What is the primary purpose of the Bible? How does an infinite Creator communicate with finite creatures? Can we learn scientific facts or theories from the Bible? What is the difference between *inspiration* and *interpretation*, with respect to the Bible? How (if at all) can science help us interpret the Bible? How are science and theology related? A guided discussion of questions such as these, using a text that students have read carefully enough to answer specific questions accurately, can only help students engage the issues of our own day with analytical rigor and genuine openness to new points of view.

Future Challenges: The Need for an Interdisciplinary Conversation

The biggest challenges related to teaching science at a Christian college undoubtedly come from evolution. Many of our students attend churches that not only reject biological evolution, but are also strongly committed to interpreting early Genesis "literally," such that modern scientific conclusions about the great age of the earth and the universe (approximately 4.6 billion years and 13.7 billion years, respectively) are categorically denied or even seen as heretical. The emphasis on a "recent" creation (no more than 10-12,000 years) is itself relatively recent, having been widely endorsed by conservative Protestants only since the rise of "scientific creationism" in the 1960s. However, the common descent of humans and other organisms—the central idea of evolution—has never been embraced by a significant percentage of conservative Protestants. Students who enroll in a course about "science and religion" at Christian colleges typically expect the course not only to focus on issues related to origins, but also to defend and promote an anti-evolutionary view— whether or not those expectations are appropriate. As institutions, individual Christian colleges might or might not have formal policies about the specific view(s) that faculty may hold and teach. As a result, it is never easy to address origins adequately, and any workable solution will have to keep this in mind.

Historically, the relationship between conservative Protestants and science has involved considerable tension and ambivalence; this no less true for those who identify as "evangelicals," whom I will mainly address in this section, than for those who call themselves "fundamentalists." On the one hand, evangelicals usually embrace the findings of science with enthusiasm, when it comes to most applications in medicine and engineering. Evangelicals also fully accept the demonstrated results of the experimental sciences, such as physics, chemistry, physiology, and thermodynamics. They have no problems with gravitation, the periodic table, the circulation of the blood, or the law of entropy. Here, their attitude is highly empirical: if it can be shown from repeatable experiments and observations, it is true and therefore does not challenge Christianity.

On the other hand, evangelicals are hesitant to accept some conclusions of the so-called historical sciences, such as geology, cosmology, paleontology, and evolutionary biology. Fundamentalists flatly reject the very legitimacy of those sciences; they have created their own alternative explanation, "creation science," which comports with their particular views of biblical authority and hermeneutics.[23] Evangelicals as a group are more ambivalent. Many evangelicals accept the big bang and modern geology, with an ancient earth and a long history of living things before humans arrived on the planet—indeed, quite a few (including some leading advocates of "intelligent design") believe that aspects of the big bang theory strongly support belief in the divine creation of the universe. Common descent, however, remains a very serious problem for many evangelicals, motivating them to look for alternative views. Some embrace scientific creationism, while others prefer "old-earth creationism" or "progressive creationism," such as the position espoused by astronomer-apologist Hugh Ross, director of the influential ministry Reasons to Believe (www.reasons.org). A significant number of evangelicals probably prefer intelligent design (ID), a position that (at least officially) takes no stance on the age of the earth and universe, although most ID proponents have no quarrel with mainstream science on those issues. Technically, ID has no stance on human evolution, either: as long as "design" can be shown *from and within science itself*, evolution is acceptable to ID advocates, in theory. In practice, however, many ID leaders have said strongly negative things about evolution (which is often called "Darwinism"), including "theistic evolution," leading most observers to conclude that ID is just another form of antievolutionism, albeit the most sophisticated form that has yet appeared.

Many evangelicals do not see any viable way to combine human evolution with the following beliefs, which they see as crucial to Christian faith: the uniqueness of humans, who alone bear the "image of God"; the actual ("historical") fall of Adam and Eve, the original parents of all humans, from a sinless state, by their own free choices to disobey God; the responsibility of each person for their own actions and beliefs, within a universe that is not fully deterministic; and the redemption of individual persons by the atoning sacrifice of Christ. Given the great significance of these beliefs, the sixty-four-dollar question is: can evangelicals maintain those beliefs without simultaneously affirming the necessity of a historical, separately created first human pair?

I doubt that evangelicals will ever fully embrace evolution if this question is not answered to their satisfaction. Traditional understandings of the *imago dei* and the fall are closely related to the view that the early chapters of Genesis are at least loosely historical, not mythical or some other non-historical literary genré. Many finer points of evangelical theology are linked with the historicity of Adam and Eve.

Thus, if evangelicals are to be persuaded to accept human evolution, it must come about by theological rather than scientific persuasion. Furthermore, any such efforts must clearly reaffirm and maintain core evangelical beliefs about the dignity, sinfulness, and responsibility of each and every human being. Evangelical theologians and biblical scholars may hold the trump cards in this conversation. If several were to be persuaded that the scientific evidence for evolution is sufficiently strong to warrant a re-examination of the traditional interpretation, then it may be possible to harmonize a credible gospel with credible science. However, recent efforts by some leading evangelical scientists and scholars to promote conversation about this issue have not been well received, and in some cases individuals have been dismissed from academic positions or been investigated for theological unorthodoxy.[24]

At the present time, there is an enormous gap between popular conceptions of scientific conclusions, methods, and attitudes, and those of scientists themselves, including most evangelical scientists. This gap is not unique to science among practitioners of specialized knowledge, and it is not unique to evangelicals among the lay public. But it is real and very significant, and it affects theologians and biblical scholars no less than anyone else. In Galileo's day, it was the scientists who eventually convinced the theologians and biblical scholars to accept Copernicus' theory of the earth's motion around the sun, but it took a long time. The process was difficult and often painful. We might be in a similar situation today.

If this is an accurate assessment, then how should faculty at evangelical colleges approach this particular aspect of the relationship between science and religion? In my opinion, two things must be kept in mind. First, faculty need to *respect* the beliefs of their students, while at the same time students must *expect* to be able to explain their views clearly and to defend them carefully against alternative views that they can also explain clearly. It can be effective to introduce students to multiple models, including scientific creationism, progressive creation, intelligent design, and theistic evolution, without too strongly favoring any one model, in order that students are encouraged to compare ideas objectively and think for themselves. We have done this at Messiah for decades, and faculty elsewhere are doing similar things.[25]

Second, we need to recognize that the conversation about science and religion is considerably broader and richer now than it was around the time of the *Scopes* trial in 1925, when current evangelical attitudes were still forming. At that time, American Protestants faced a very grim choice. On the one hand, they could follow politician William Jennings Bryan and the fundamentalists, rejecting modern science in the name of biblical authority and orthodox beliefs. On the other hand, they could follow theologian Shailer Mathews and the liberal Protestants, who called themselves "modernists," rejecting biblical authority and orthodox beliefs in the name of modern science. At the height of the controversy, Bryan asked a famous Christian artist, Ernest James Pace, to draw a cartoon depicting the religious consequences of accepting evolution (below). It shows "three well-dressed modernists going down" a staircase, on which "there is no stopping place"—a slippery slope from "Christianity" at the top to "Atheism" at the bottom. Along the way, they abandon their belief in miracles, the virgin birth, the deity of Jesus, the atonement, and the resurrection.[26]

Quite a few "modernist" Christians from Bryan's day fit this picture rather well; although most of them did not become agnostics or atheists, they did take the other steps, largely in the name of science.[27] Quite a few contemporary Christians, including Peacocke and Haught, also seem to conform to this pattern; they are in effect intellectual and spiritual descendents of the modernists from the 1920s. However, today there is a new feature on the landscape that cannot be ignored: a significant number of top scientists who accept evolution without descending Bryan's staircase. There was no one like them in the 1920s, and the conversation then was consequently more highly polarized. The most influential member of this group is probably John Polkinghorne, a distinguished English mathematical physicist who gave up his chair at Cambridge at the zenith of his career to become an Anglican priest. Unlike those who have gone down Bryan's steps, Polkinghorne unambiguously affirms the Nicene Creed in his aptly titled book, *The Faith of a Physicist*, and in other works he advances a robust argument from design alongside a full acceptance of evolution.[28] Others in this group (to name just a few) include Nobel Laureate for physics William Phillips, geneticist Francis Collins, astrophysicist Joan Centrella, astronomer and historian Owen Gingerich, paleontologist Simon Conway Morris, neuroscientist William Newsome, and nuclear engineer Ian Hutchinson. All of these people are excellent scientists, and they all believe in the divinity of Jesus, the bodily resurrection, and the actual divine creation of the universe—contradicting Bryan's fears. Students at evangelical colleges ought to be introduced to at least some of them.

Ultimately, faculty at each institution will make their own decisions whether to teach students about Christianity and science, how to go about it, and where to house it in the curriculum. No two institutional contexts are identical, and no two faculty members will bring the same professional preparation into the classroom. If we do not take up the challenge of teaching our students about this topic, however, then in my opinion we are failing to educate them for one of the strongest challenges they will face as Christians in the modern world.

APPENDIX

An assignment to prepare students for a discussion of a crucial text related to science and Christianity: Galileo Galilei (1564-1642), *Letter to the Grand Duchess Christina, Concerning the Use of Biblical Quotations in Matters of Science* (1615).

Introduction

In 1543 Nicolaus Copernicus, a minor official of the Catholic Church in his native Poland, published his famous book, *On the Revolutions of the Heavenly Orbs*, in which he argued that the earth goes around the sun and not *vice versa*. But the notion that the earth is hurtling around the sun at thousands of miles an hour while spinning on its axis once a day stands in clear opposition to our everyday experience—if we're really going that fast, why can't we tell? Why don't we fly off the earth, as mud flies off a rotating wheel? Why aren't clouds and flying birds left behind by the rapid motion of the earth's surface? These and other objections drawn from common sense, from physical theories of the day, and even from astronomy itself, prevented most Europeans from endorsing the radical ideas of Copernicus. For quite a few people, however, the most serious objections were theological. In a number of places the Bible speaks of the motion of the sun and/or the immobility of the earth (some such passages are Josh 10:12-14; Ps 19:4-6, 93:-1, and 104:5; Is 38:8; Eccles 1:5). Most Protestant and Catholic theologians therefore assumed quite naturally that the Scriptures bore witness to the truth of the same geocentric system that most scientists of their day took to be the true picture of the universe.

Copernicanism, then, was a minority opinion for many years after the publication of Copernicus' book. Not until 1609-10, when Galileo Galilei turned a telescope on the heavens, was there forthcoming any new evidence that favored the heliocentric system of Copernicus over the geocentric system of the ancient Greek scientists Aristotle and Ptolemy. What Galileo saw with his telescope—the phases of Venus, the moons of Jupiter, spots on the sun and mountains on the moon—could not be reconciled with the Ptolemaic system of the world. Always an eager polemicist, Galileo rushed into print with his discoveries. In *The Starry*

Messenger, published in March 1610, less than eight months after he had first heard of a telescope, Galileo recounted his observations and identified the sun as the center of the universe.

Although Galileo had not discussed theology in any way, he was soon attacked by certain conservative priests who saw his views as threatening the received interpretation of Scripture. The reaction against Protestantism was already in full swing; it was not a good time to challenge the authority of the Church. Seeing the need to defend Copernicanism from the charge of impiety, Galileo penned a long position paper, in the form of an open letter to Christina of Lorraine, mother of Galileo's patron Cosimo II de' Medici, the Grand Duke of Tuscany. The Grand Duchess, who was skeptical of the new ideas, had asked Galileo's friend, the Benedictine monk Benedetto Castelli, whether Copernican views were suitable for a good Catholic. In drafting his reply, Galileo relied heavily on St. Augustine, who had cautioned Christians not to take literally those portions of the Bible that dealt with astronomy: wishing to convey spiritual truths to the faithful, who were usually unlearned, the Holy Spirit had employed popular language that was not meant to be scientifically correct.

In his letter, Galileo used this Augustinian notion of accommodation to argue that Copernicanism is not heretical merely because it goes against the unadorned meaning of certain Scriptural passages. He also pointed out that heliocentrism had been proposed by a good Catholic (Copernicus), who had published his views at the encouragement of important Church officials.

Questions for students to answer in writing, prior to coming to class:
The questions below are designed to accompany the translation in *Discoveries and Opinions of Galileo*, by Stillman Drake (Garden City, NY: Doubleday, 1957). If another translation is substituted, then the questions based on Drake's lengthy introduction must be omitted.

Drake's Introduction to Galileo's Letter to the Grand Duchess (Drake, pp. 145-71)

1. What circumstances led Galileo to write his letter to the Grand Duchess?

2. What principles or rules did Galileo hold regarding the purpose and interpretation of the Bible? List them.

3. What principles or rules did Robert Bellarmine hold regarding the purpose and interpretation of the Bible? List them. How did he want Galileo and others to treat the Copernican theory?

4. Whom (Galileo or Bellarmine) do *you* agree with more? Be specific about your reasons.

Galileo, Letter to the Grand Duchess Christina (Drake, pp. 173-216)

1. What does Galileo believe in general concerning the language of scripture? What does he believe specifically about the use of the Bible in matters of science? What principle(s) of interpretation does he endorse, and why?

2. What does Galileo believe about the nature, scope, and relative certainty/ambiguity of scientific knowledge? What limitations (if any) does he place on science?

3. What does he believe about the nature, scope, and relative certainty/ambiguity of theological knowledge? What limitations (if any) does he place on theology?

4. In this essay, Galileo employs at least three different metaphorical models to describe the relation between science and faith: the "two books/harmony" model (theology and science in agreement), the "separation" model (theology and science as dealing with different things), and the "handmaiden" model (theology as "queen" and science as "handmaiden"). Identify where he discusses each (listing page numbers), and summarize what he says about each.

5. How do *you* respond to Galileo: what do you like about his position (and why), what do you have reservations about (and why)?

Alternative assignment involving excerpts from Galileo's *Letter*

Instructors who want to assign only a portion of this text can still use some of the questions without modification. For a shorter assignment that still includes many of the most important ideas, assign just the following selection (as paginated in Drake):

- the first three paragraphs on 175-6
- from the start of 177 through the top of 179
- from the second full paragraph on 180 ("Such are the people . . .") through the first full paragraph on 183
- from the bottom of 199 through the middle of 202
   - from the bottom of 205 through the top of 211

In this case, use only these questions:

1. What does Galileo say about the language of the Bible, *in general*?
2. What does he say specifically about Biblical references *to scientific phenomena*?
3. What does Galileo want the theologians to do, all things considered?
4. What do *you* think of Galileo's approach to Biblical texts relating to nature. What (if anything) do you like? What (if anything) do you not like?

Chapter 7 Notes

1. Peter Holmes, trans., *On Prescription Against Heretics*, in *The Ante-Nicene Fathers*, eds. Alexander Roberts and James Donaldson (New York: Scribners, 1896-1903), iii, 246.

2. Henri-Irénée Marrou, *History of Education in Antiquity* (London: Sheed and Ward, 1956), 316.

3. As quoted by Sydney Ross, "*Scientist*: The Story of a Word," *Annals of Science* 18 (1962): 65-85, on 71-72, emphasis in the original. Ross quotes Whewell's anonymous review of Mary Somerville's book, *On the Connexion of the Physical Sciences* (London: John Murray, 1834), in *The Quarterly Review* 51 (1834): 58-61.

4. Here I have borrowed a little from my essay, "Science as Christian Vocation: The Case of Robert Boyle," in *Reading God's World: The Scientific Vocation*, ed. Angus J. L. Menuge (St. Louis: Concordia Publishing House, 2004), 189-210.

5. Royal Society, Boyle Papers, vol. 44, fol. 95. Michael Hunter has made this text available at http://www.livesandletters.ac.uk/wd/view/text_dip/WD1_dip.html. For more on this aspect of Boyle, see Edward B. Davis, "Robert Boyle's Religious Life, Attitudes, and Vocation," *Science & Christian Belief* 19.2 (2007): 117-38.

6. Multiple versions of this quotation are attributed to Holmes, but I have been unable to confirm a specific version or to confirm its authenticity.

7. C. P. Snow, *The Two Cultures* (Cambridge: Cambridge University Press, 1959).

8. John Brooke and Geoffrey Cantor, *Reconstructing Nature: The Engagement of Science and Religion* (Edinburgh: T. & T. Clark, 1998), 47-57.

9. For detailed studies of six prominent examples, see Karl Giberson and Mariano Artigas, *Oracles of Science: Celebrity Scientists Versus God and Religion* (New York: Oxford University Press, 2007).

10. John William Draper, *History of the Conflict between Religion and Science* (New York: D. Appleton and Company, 1874), vi.

11. Andrew Dickson White, *A History of the Warfare of Science with Theology in Christendom*, 2 vols. (New York: D. Appleton and Company, 1896), 1: v-vi.

12. Michael D. Gordin and Karl Hall, "Introduction: Intelligentsia Science Inside and Outside Russia," *Osiris* 23 (2008): 1-19, on 3.

13. Stephen Jay Gould, *Rocks of Ages: Science and Religion in the Fullness of Life* (New York: Ballantine, 1999), quoting 100-101 and 5.

14. It is instructive to note (for example) that White's book is available as a free download at www.infidels.org and Draper's book at www.positiveatheism.org.

15. I originally made this point in Edward B. Davis, "Appreciating a Scientist-Theologian: Some Remarks on the Work of John Polkinghorne," *Zygon* 35.4 (December 2000): 971-976, which was written before I saw Gould's book.

16. Arthur Peacocke, *Theology for a Scientific Age*, enlarged edition (Minneapolis: Fortress Press, 1993), 22 and 268-289.

17. Haught's testimony is transcribed at <http://www.aclupa.org/downloads/Day5pmsession.pdf>, accessed 10 February 2011.

18. John Haught, *Science and Religion: From Conflict to Conversation* (New York: Paulist Press, 1995).

19. David Ray Griffin, *Religion and Scientific Naturalism: Overcoming the Conflicts* (Albany, NY: The State University of New York Press, 2000), 183, his italics, which

are meant here to contrast theology with religion, something that White also had done.

20. For a highly accessible summary of the shortcomings of the conflict thesis, see *Galileo Goes to Jail and Other Myths about Science and Religion*, ed. Ronald L. Numbers (Cambridge: Harvard University Press, 2009); a more scholarly account by David C. Lindberg and Ronald L. Numbers, "Beyond War and Peace: A Reappraisal of the Encounter between Christianity and Science," *Perspectives on Science and Christian Faith* 39 (1987): 140-149, is no less helpful.

21. Colin A. Russell, "The Conflict of Science and Religion," in *Science & Religion: A Historical Introduction*, ed. Gary B. Ferngren (Baltimore: The Johns Hopkins University Press, 2002), 10.

22. I base this on an examination of catalogs and conversations with faculty from many Christian colleges and universities. Because I do not want to criticize any specific institutions, I will not provide specific documentation.

23. For more on creationism and the historical sciences, see Edward B. Davis and Elizabeth Chmielewski, "Galileo and the Garden of Eden: Historical Reflections on Creationist Hermeneutics," in *Nature and Scripture in the Abrahamic Religions: 1700-Present*, eds. Jitse M. van der Meer and Scott H. Mandelbrote, 2 vols. (Leiden and Boston: Brill Academic Publishers, 2008), 2:437-464.

24. Richard N. Ostling, "The Search for the Historical Adam," *Christianity Today* 55.6 (June 2011): 23-27, accurately surveys the current conversation; the editors advise caution in "No Adam, No Eve, No Gospel: The historical Adam debate won't be resolved tomorrow, so stay engaged," *ibid.*, 61. For an authoritative effort to deal substantively with the theological problems posed by human evolution, see Peter Enns, *The Evolution of Adam: What the Bible Does and Doesn't Say about Human Origins* (Grand Rapids, MI: Brazos Press, 2012).

25. Messiah's approach was badly misrepresented by Marvin Olasky, "Riding the Rapids: Grand Canyon Rocks Challenge Christian Colleges' Divergent Stands on Evolution," *World* (September 11, 2010): 39-45. For information about courses at other Christian institutions, including a Jesuit high school in Ireland, see Sean M. Cordry, "Six Easy Pieces: One Pedagogical Approach to Integrating Science/Faith/Origins into College-Level Introductory Physics Courses," *Perspectives on Science and Christian Faith* 59 (2007): 268-274; Amalee Meehan, "Paradise Regained: Teaching Science from a Christian Standpoint in a Postmodern Age," *Perspectives on Science and Christian Faith* 59 (2007): 275-282; Craig A. Boyd, "Using Galileo to Teach Darwin: A Developmental and Historical Approach," *Perspectives on Science and Christian Faith* 59 (2007): 283-288; and Stephen O. Moshier, Dean Arnold, Larry L. Funck, Raymond Lewis, Albert J. Smith, John H. Walton, and William P. Wharton, "Theories of Origins: A Multi- and Interdisciplinary Course for Undergraduates at Wheaton College," *Perspectives on Science and Christian Faith* 59 (2007): 289-296.

26. This cartoon was originally published as the frontispiece in William Jennings Bryan, *Seven Questions in Dispute* (New York: Revell, 1924). Bryan's description of the cartoon is quoted by James R. Moore, *The Future of Science and Belief: Theological Views in the Twentieth Century* (Milton Keynes: The Open University Press, 1981), 40.

27. For some representative examples, see Edward B. Davis, "Fundamentalist Cartoons, Modernist Pamphlets, and the Religious Image of Science in the Scopes

Era," in *Religion and the Culture of Print in Modern America*, eds. Charles L. Cohen and Paul S. Boyer (Madison, WI: University of Wisconsin Press, 2008), 175-198.

28. John C. Polkinghorne, *From Physicist to Priest: An Autobiography* (London: Society for Promoting Christian Knowledge, 2007); *The Faith of a Physicist: Reflections of a Bottom-Up Thinker* (Princeton, NJ: Princeton University Press, 1994); *Belief in God in an Age of Science* (New Haven, CT: Yale University Press, 1998).

BEYOND THE DISCIPLINES, GOD

The Study of the Christian Scriptures and the Formation of a Faithful Habitus for Truthful Learning

John W. Wright

The current general education curriculum of the American university hovers between its encyclopedic origins and its genealogical negation.[1] As encyclopedic, we offer classes, particularly classes in the natural sciences, where students learn "a single framework within which knowledge is discriminated from mere belief, progress towards knowledge is mapped, and truth is understood as the relationship of *our* knowledge to *the* world, through the application of those methods whose rules are the rules of rationality as such."[2] Students discover a pragmatic unity to the curriculum, spelled out in the late nineteenth and early twentieth century by the American psychologist/philosopher William James. According to the Jamesian image, the university offers the student various scientistic disciplinary rooms within an educational hotel.[3] A hallway connects the rooms through doorways, i.e., rationality as such. Students may enter rooms to sample various domains of study selectively, perhaps in order to choose one for lifelong professional or recreational consumption; more likely they rush through to get the visit "out of the way."

As genealogical, we require students to leave the hallway to enter other disciplinary rooms, particularly the social sciences and the humanities. Students enter these disciplines through previously unseen apertures in order to undo a unitary concept of reason. In these rooms, students learn that there is "a multiplicity of perspectives within each of which truth-from-a-point-of-view may be asserted, but no truth-as-such, an empty notion, about *the* world, an equally empty notion. There are no rules of rationality as such to be appealed to, there are rather strategies of insight and strategies of subversion."[4] These rooms form socially engaged rationalities. Here students learn to make a difference in the world, to provide a voice for the voiceless, and to empower those oppressed by the dominant hegemonic powers. In these rooms students learn the moral and political superiority of resistance over hegemony. Students become strategic, activist intellects to unsettle the settled, to denaturalize the natural, to learn to engage in authentic and meaningful activities either professionally as an activist or as a volunteer within the civil society of their choice.

In such a curriculum bifurcated between nature and culture, students learn most of all that there is a hallway, a respite outside the conflict of the faculty. The hallway stands beyond the gaze of professors, monitored by the coercive discipline of the local university administration and the state. The marketplace governs this realm to provide entertainment, fun, and a lever to release pressure from the stress of the classroom. From the students' perspective, it seems a realm of peace. No conflict is visibly manifest as market-formed demographic niches lead students into parallel passages in the market-formed width of the hallway. When conflicts do emerge, the administration and/or state moves quickly to expunge its evidence from historical consciousness to restore the university's and state's desired image as the arbitrators of peace.

The general education curricular structure mirrors the larger institutional conflict within the contemporary university faculty. Particular academic disciplines exist through the force of the encyclopedic tradition. Students learn, as their faculty before them, to control and dominate nature, to manage and produce for profit within the neoliberal marketplace. Cultural studies and related modes of thought exist parasitically upon this work of productivity. The faculty of resistance legitimate themselves through the criticism of the neo-liberal forces that reduce knowledge to productivity, masking the deep interests already embedded in the categories of the knowledge produced. The university provides the field of dreams upon which the faculty and students participate in the agonistic dialectic of hegemony and resistance. The university *qua* university transforms the struggle into the creative production of history. The university forms students to "make a difference" as intentional players within the production of history. Students learn to manage the conflict between hegemony and resistance with technical competence, to express their own will in order to judge when to dominate and when to resist. Most of all, they learn to escape into the hallway of relationships (or hooking up) to consume material or cultural goods or each other; such a realm is ultimately much more fun than struggle.

How does one place the study of God, theology, in such a setting? The question disrupts. Is it a matter of hegemony or resistance? Knowledge or faith? Learning or values clarification? A single room or the hallway? The fact that the question disrupts shows how deeply the modern/postmodern university has formed us. Perhaps we might turn to a foundational text of the contemporary university—Immanuel Kant's *The Conflict of the Faculties*—in order to understand better the tacit knowledge that shapes our daily work and life.

Kant, the University, and the Discipline of the State

Immanuel Kant, the eighteenth-century Prussian Enlightenment philosopher, is famous for his three philosophical critiques—*The Critique of Pure Reason*, *The Critique of Practical Reason*, and *The Critique of Judgment*—and his important essay, "What Is Enlightenment?" Nonetheless, as Thomas Howard has noted, another of Kant's essays, "The Conflict of the Faculties,"

> is a work of rich significance. Not only does it shed light on Kant's personal religious views, but the work also effectively summed up, while adding trenchant commentary to, the growing concern many had about the division of the faculties. What is more, the work influenced many future directions of German

university development: practically every major figure involved in the founding of the University of Berlin would have known its contents and the circumstances of its writing quite well.[5]

Kant's essay provides a genealogical foundation for the transformation of universities that occurred in the United States during the late nineteenth and twentieth centuries.

The deepest presupposition of Kant's essay is the universality of the state. As Jacques Derrida rightly notes, for Kant the university

> is not authorized by itself. It is authorized (*berechtigt*) by a non-university agency—here, by the state—and according to criteria no longer necessarily or finally those of scientific competence, but those of a certain performativity. The autonomy of scientific evaluation may be absolute and unconditioned, but the political effects of its legitimation, even supposing that one could in all rigor distinguish them, are nonetheless controlled, measured, and overseen by a power outside the university.[6]

The state grounds the university as the condition for its existence.

The higher faculty, the faculty of theology, law, and medicine, operate directly under the state to provide an educated class to manage its populace: "the following order exists among the incentives that the government can use to achieve its end (of influencing the people)."[7] Even though Kant emphasizes the absolute autonomy of the "lower faculty" from state interference, this faculty still exists for the state. As the "lower" philosophy faculty pursues its disinterested, rational research, the higher faculty mediates the lower faculty's findings to the state bureaucracy:

> The result of the freedom, which the philosophy faculty must enjoy unimpaired, is that the higher faculties (themselves better instructed) will lead these officials more and more onto the way of truth. And the officials, of their own part, also more enlightened about their duty, will not be repelled at changing their exposition, since the new way involves nothing more than a clearer insight into means for achieving the same end.[8]

The state provides the end, the *telos*, of the university. The state is the university's Alpha and Omega, its beginning and end, the context in which the university lives and moves and has its being. For Kant, the university performs for the state as the state calls it into existence.

As part of the higher faculty, the theology faculty, what Kant calls "biblical theologians," serves the state both directly and indirectly. Directly, the Bible possesses a utilitarian worth to aid the state's domination of its population:

> . . . the Bible deserves to be kept, put to moral use, and assigned to religion as its guide *just as if it is a divine revelation.*
>
> If the government were to neglect that great means for establishing and administering civil order and peace and abandon it to frivolous hands, the audacity of those prodigies of strength who imagine they have already outgrown this leading-string of dogma . . . would soon make it [the state] regret its indulgence.[9]

Kant's vision is not merely a Constantinian modernity where theology works to legitimate the morality of the nation-state; it is what Thomas Howard calls an "Erastian modernity": "a process whereby the churches were virtually annexed to the modernizing state and subjected to major government oversight and regulation."[10] The theology faculty's direct subordination to the state was their price of admission into Kant's university.

Indirectly, the theology faculty serves the state by mediating conflict between the state and the lower faculty. While the theology faculty may not criticize the work of the philosophy faculty, the philosophy faculty disciplines the theology faculty according to the "critique of reason."[11] The theology faculty must re-state its teachings in light of reason, the work of the lower faculty: "when conflict arises about the sense of a scriptural text, philosophy—that is, the lower faculty, which has truth as its end—claims the prerogative of deciding its meaning."[12] For instance, as "the only thing that matters in religion is *deeds*, and this final aim, accordingly, a meaning appropriate to it, must be attributed to every biblical dogma."[13] Therefore, "ecclesiastical faith, as the mere vehicle of religious faith, is mutable and must remain open to gradual purification until it coincides with religious faith."[14] The study of the Bible within the university necessarily involves a task of correlation, constantly adjusting the ecclesial faith to bring it into line with universal reason and morality. Then the theology faculty may transmit it to state officials who shape the populace to bring about "peace and harmony" for the state. Reason, seen in the bodies of the philosophy faculty, must discipline theology, seen in the bodies of the theology faculty, for the good of the state. Kant's university and its disciplines regulate, control, and neutralize the theology faculty through state authority and philosophical, scientific reason. Theology possesses no authority of its own; it exists for mediation in terms provided by other disciplines.

The Habitus of the Discipline of the Conflict of Faculties

It is tempting to read Kant's essay like Jacques Derrida: "Reading him today, I perceive his assurance and his necessity much as one might admire the rigor of a plan or structure through the breaches of an uninhabitable edifice, unable to decide whether it is in ruins or simply never existed, having only ever been able to shelter the discourse of its non-accomplishment."[15] Kant's confidence in pure reason and a paternalistic, benevolent state makes his vision sound as archaic as the alchemist's lab.

Yet it is not difficult to find ourselves within the Kantian tradition of the university, even at a private Christian university. The tendency to focus general education theology classes as descriptive classes on "the Bible" per se reflects the enduring Kantian legacy. The Christian university's curricular and extra-curricular concern with biblical morality, whether to teach the students "personal righteousness" or "social justice," already reflects the Kantian categories that abstract the Scriptures from its proper locus in the church. The sense among Christian university faculty that the university needs to mediate the "objective knowledge" drawn from their own disciplines in order to deepen the church's effectiveness repeats the same Kantian legacy. Departments of Religion (the Kantian term for the universal human phenomenon of which theology is a particular instance) still face pressure to translate Christian doctrine into a philosophical language already intelligible to the culture for their students. The list could go on. Yet I would like to argue that the modern/

postmodern university more deeply complicates our task by forming disciplinary habits, or more precisely, a habitus, that render problematic the teaching of theology for our students' general education.

Pierre Bourdieau, the French sociologist, re-habilitates the medieval concept of habitus in his *Outline of a Theory of Practice.* The concept allows Bourdieau to show how social "structures" become repeated and encoded in human bodies and behavior without reifying such structures. For Bourdieau, a habitus is

> systems of durable, transposable *dispositions*, structured structures predisposed to function as structuring structures, that is, as principles of the generation and structuring of practices and representations which can be objectively "regulated" and "regular" without in any way being the product of obedience to rules, objectively adapted to their goals without presupposing a conscious aiming at ends or an express mastery of the operations necessary to attain them and, being all this, collectively orchestrated without being the product of the orchestrating action of a conductor.[16]

More simply put, a habitus is "the durably installed generative principle of regulated improvisations" or even more simply, "history turned into nature."[17] Through the concept of habitus, Bourdieau allows us to overcome the subjectivist/objectivist dichotomy of human agency in order to "establish an experimental science of the *dialectic of the internalization of externality and the externalization of internality.*"[18] Within a university setting, we might describe the habitus as the outcome of the disciplinary structures that generate a student's general education—the fundamental shaping, not of particular curricular choices or information, but the conditions that make such curricular choices possible.

Students receive their habitus, their general education, within the disciplinary structures of the modern university with its Kantian legacy. First, students learn the rules of managing conflict for and under the authority of the state. The Kantian university confines the conflict of the faculties to a designated space within the university so as not to disturb the state in its hegemony over its people, even as the university actively serves the state. Derrida argues that Kant's university is "as much a safeguard for the most totalitarian of social forms as a place for the most intransigently liberal resistance to any abuse of power, resistance that can be judged in turns as most rigorous or most impotent."[19] In either case, the state is the reality that one must support or oppose. The university forms a habitus in students that presupposes that the state is the chief political actor and authorizer of human goods. The university's discipline makes such a history nature for general education: responsibility in strategic relations within and for the state becomes the most fundamental habitus of the university.

The Kantian structures form students into an even more differentiated habitus. The university reinforces the liberal democratic distinction between the public and the private realms, which are "two quite separate conceptual realms: one in which unquestioned obedience to authority prevails (the juridical definitions upheld by the state); the other consisting of rational argument and exchange, in which authority has no place (the omnicompetence of criticism)."[20] Through their transformation within late capitalism, we find these realms encoded into the university as what Robert Bellah calls the two realms of American culture, the managerial and the therapeutic.[21] Bellah himself developed these categories from Alasdair MacIntyre's explication of the role of the manager and the therapist:

> The manager represents in his character the obliteration of the distinction between manipulative and nonmanipulative social relations; the therapist represents the same obliteration in the sphere of personal life. The manager treats ends as given, as outside his scope; his concern is with technique, with effectiveness in transforming raw materials into final products, unskilled labor into skilled labor, investments into profits. The therapist also treats ends as given, as outside his scope; his concern also is with technique, with effectiveness in transforming neurotic symptoms into directed energy, maladjusted individuals into well-adjusted ones.[22]

These realms become encoded in the university in the distinction between the "rooms" and the "hallway" of the university. Rooms are governed by a judicial reason overseen by the faculty—students must learn "what the professor wants"; the free rationality of consumerism, the ability to choose what one desires, governs the hallway.

The university forms its students into these realms through a menu approach to general education. Students are habituated into moving in and through authoritative rationalities in their various classrooms where they alternate between hegemonic and resistant judicial reason. The classroom forms students into a habitus of negotiation, "a politics of the negotiating party, with every work negotiating even as it states a premise or a theory."[23] Such a formation prepares students to enter the "system of professions" that await most upon their terminal academic degree.[24]

More significantly, however, students distinguish this judicial rationality from the more "universal" realm of the free rationality of the consumer. The hallway provides the ability, the "freedom," to choose their own values and meaning outside the realm of judicial reason. Combined, such networks form a habitus to prepare the students to enter the negotiated realms of the professions, while balancing this realm with the private realm of personal meaning and therapeutic activities such as family and church.

These forces are not unique to the university; they form the basic disciplinary fabric of life within a liberal-democratic polity. Students enter the university with this habitus already ingrained within their bodies. The general education of the university deepens the internalization and permanence of such a habitus. The university formation often occurs simultaneously as young adults undergo a social redefinition in movement away from the local, concrete commitments to the abstract commitments necessary to sustain a liberal society.[25] This habitus, however, makes theology, the knowledge of God, fundamentally problematic in general education for the students. Instead of language about God and all things related to God, theology becomes the realm of "personal values."

First, the habitus inculcated by the contemporary university structures education with the state as its beginning and end. God, at best, becomes an interesting "hypothesis" within the given realm of existence, unnecessary to the workings of the society and world, and therefore, outside the realm of knowledge. Faith becomes separate from knowledge; revelation contrary to rationality rather than its basis; the good becomes "values." Ironically, the nation-state becomes more basic in defining life than God.

Theology has a name for such a habitus: it's called idolatry. Christians, along with Jews and Muslims, have generally understood idolatry as irrational. Idolatry stands as a (in)substantial obstacle to the study of God as part of students' general education.

Second, and relatedly, the habitus formed in students presupposes that the state is the most significant political actor in the world rather than the church. Human activities are weighed in relationship to their impact within the state rather than constancy of witness within the church. To "make a difference in the world" requires the virtues of the politics of the state such as responsibility, efficiency, compromise, control, and toleration rather than the Christian virtues of faith, hope, and love. Involvement in local congregations becomes voluntary and largely irrelevant except for private enrichment or communal social activism. The university habituates students into a system that sees the state, not the church, as significant for human life and activity.

Such a habitus renders theology unintelligible. Theology quickly becomes vacuous when abstracted from the practices that its language supports. Jesus did not institute the liberal nation-state on the night when he was betrayed, but the church, through giving his disciples bread and the cup, his body and blood. Theology presupposes the life of the church catholic, the communion of saints through the ages. It is the language of this particular people that God has called into existence through the life of the Jews and especially the life, death, and resurrection of Jesus Christ. Before theology can even become intelligible as a discourse of knowledge, the students need to be re-formed from the implicit Erastian commitments of the modern university. Knowledge of God requires participation by faith within the church, for theological knowledge always has its beginning and end in Love, the Love that is the Triune God that is revealed to us from the Father in Jesus Christ by the power of the Holy Spirit.

Third, the habitus formed by the structures of the university compartmentalizes theology into specific categories that profoundly distort its discourse. Placed into the private realm of the therapeutic, theology becomes, as Christian Smith has shown, a discourse of moralistic

therapeutic deism, or better, of a moralistic therapeutic relational deity—
"a divine butler and cosmic therapist."[26] Theology becomes about significance rather than truth, human experience rather than God. Moreover,
the one-class-one-subject-one-grade structure habituates students to
expect that theology is about a particular subject or object in the world.
The university structures themselves tend to reduce God to an Object
among objects or a Being among beings. Such structures distort language about God, itself a very tricky matter. While theology is knowledge of God and all things in relationship to God, we know God only as
One Unknown, as Thomas Aquinas reminds us. We know God through
God's effects, that is, through creation, particularly the human, Jesus
Christ, and then all things through Him. Language about God does
not refer to a subject to be mastered or an object to be analyzed and
controlled; language about God requires a particular use of language
that implicates all language. It is ultimately the language of prayer and
praise. God implodes the categories of the managerial and therapeutic
and exceeds any language of subject or object. The compartmental-
izing habitus of students, formed by the university, restricts the ability
to include theology into a general education curriculum without severe
problems.

Finally, the categorization of theology as a distinct academic subject
places theology within the same mediating role as endorsed by Kant.
The habitus of the modern university seeks to relate theology as a discreet field of inquiry to parallel discreet fields of inquiry, particularly
in upper-division, capstone-type classes. It raises questions like, "How
does faith relate to science?" rather than how do we speak well of the
relationship of God to creation as seen in Jesus Christ and witnessed
to in Scriptures? Theological discourse becomes governed by the supposed rationally-determined givenness of other academic disciplines.
Correlation between "two originally distinct spheres of knowledge"
becomes the goal. Within the habitus formed by the contemporary
university, classes on "theology and psychology," "theological and
business ethics," "theology and science," and "theology and literature"
achieve a coherence based upon a mediating function of theology that
would never occur in classical Christian thought. Such classes have an
apologetic intent, a way to make "God" relevant to students' lives and

the world. As Karl Barth has taught us, however, another disciplinary "prolegomena" to which theology then relates already bears within it theological and philosophical commitments that render theological discourse problematic.[27] It replaces God's revelation in Jesus Christ with categories that are seen as "natural" or already given.

If this is so, the habitus formed by the contemporary university renders theology as a disciplinary part of a university deeply problematic. Such a university already exists under the discipline of a foundation by the state that distorts the very possibility of theological discourse. As the logic of this works its way to its end, the problem of its foundation has become readily apparent in terms of the incoherence, irrelevance, and ironically, the irrationality of the contemporary university. Perhaps Jacques Derrida is correct: "If there can be no pure concept of the university, if, within the university, there can be no pure or purely rational concept of the university, this—to speak somewhat elliptically. . . is due very simply to the fact that the university is *founded*. An event of foundation can never be comprehended merely within the logic that it founds."[28] Kant's foundation on pure rationality through the power of the modern state has failed.

Yet this failure opens up future possibilities. If, as David Burrell has suggested, the modern was the post-medieval, then we might understand the post-modern as the post-post-medieval.[29] Perhaps by returning to the medieval origins of the university we might re-discover a habitus that renders theology intelligible as a rational discourse that forms human beings to know God—and therefore the world—truthfully. Perhaps we need a general education, the formation of truthful habitus, to enable our students—and faculty—to read Scriptures as witnesses to the revelation of the triune God in whom and through whom and for whom we—and all creation—live and move and have our being.

Beyond the Disciplines, God

How does one get beyond the disciplines of the modern university to recover a habitus sufficient for theological discourse? As John Milbank has suggested, timidity will not do:

> theology, in the face of secular attack, is only on secure ground
> if it adopts the most extreme mode of counterattack: namely

that unless other disciplines are (at least implicitly) ordered to theology (assuming that this means participation in God's self-knowledge—as in the Augustinian tradition) they are objectively and demonstrably null and void, altogether lacking in truth, which to have any meaning must involve some sort of adequation (for mere "coherence" can only concern the coherence of conventions or appearances).[30]

We need, as Derrida suggests, to return to a new foundation, a foundation before/after the disciplinary function of "pure reason."

Perhaps we may find such a foundation in the origins of the Western university. According to Stephen Ferruolo, the Western university emerged as twelfth-century school masters incorporated monastic and moralistic criticism of fragmentation, pride, and ambition into an educational ideal that organized all knowledge into a unity.[31] By incorporating the monastic end of learning in the knowledge of God as fundamental to its intellectual endeavor, the university arose to form an educated habitus in its students that found its beginning and end in the love of God. It is this founding that we might repeat.

Merely cosmetic changes will not do. We must rethink the habitus of our institutions, their histories that we now accept as nature. To accomplish a medieval non-identical repetition amid our current Kantian non-identical repetition will take re-thinking our institutions and general education in light of this new/old founding. We must shift an educational habitus for faculty, administrators, and students from the cultural given in which we live to one rendering theology possible without falling into the dialectic of hegemony and resistance. It seems to me that the key to such a transition is readily available to Christian colleges and universities if we could only maximize the inherent logic of such an institution's practices. My suggestion is simply that the whole of the university's intellectual and social life culminate in the proper worship of the Triune God in chapel.[32] If students might be taught the proper craft of Christian worship, then the Spirit may bring forth the appropriate habitus, or general education, to form them to become faithful learners in seeing the world truthfully as the creation of the eternally Triune God. The institution could unite to develop students' participation in Christian worship rather than accommodating Christian worship to meet student development as defined by the liberal democratic habitus. Three steps seem mandatory.

First, the general education classroom should develop a cultural studies perspective on historic and contemporary Western university and culture as part of their "first-year" experience. If students have had their habitus formed by a toxic culture which sees war as natural and peace as unrealistic, which has taught them that university life is a means of economic exchange for fun and profit, they need to bring to consciousness, as much as possible, the tacit knowledge and underlying cultural narratives that the students, faculty, and administration have brought into the university. The students need to come to terms with the modernist co-optation of the Christian founding of the university and discover its original founding event in the love of learning as the desire for God revealed in Jesus.[33]

Having recognized their ignorance and malformation, the students need positive examples of excellence in the craft of worship—much like writing professors' assignments for the students to read excellent writing exemplars. The students need to encounter stories of experts in Christian worship, that is, the lives of the saints, those whose lives become intelligible only in light of God's revelation in Jesus Christ. Perhaps like labs in biology, students could be formed bit by bit with the skills, observations, and language necessary to participate in Christian worship. Through slow habituation of practice and the gaining of a language, students can form a habitus that expects worship to find its end in participation in the gospel through the proclamation of the Scriptures and participation in the Eucharist. Because of their malformed habitus upon arrival into the university, first-year students should receive instruction into the history and practices of the university chapel—and particularly the skills and dispositions that the expert participants in the practices need to develop. Universities regularly require prerequisites that are necessary to engage in advanced activities; Calculus II always requires the proficiency achieved by the students in Calculus I.

As part of this formation, participation in faithful local congregations, the body of Christ, under the sacramental authority of local pastors, could be explained as essential, much like membership in a choir is necessary for the first-year vocalist as she develops her craft. The local congregation, not the university, is the means by which God has elected to witness to God's own self in the world. Of course, this presupposes that the students will find the faculty, the masters, deeply embedded, faithful, and obedient in congregations in and around the university to aid them in the movement back and forth from the university chapel to the local congregation. The particular tradition of the Christian university stands in a complicated relationship to the society that surrounds it. Through allowing students to gain awareness of their placement within the university, it could provide an initial habitus to participate in the university's worship, much as early Christianity required an extended catechumenate before baptism and admittance of the believer into the fullness of the Christian rites.[34]

Second, the university must return the primary locus of theological discourse to its proper place: the worship of the church. In chapel, the university becomes visibly manifest as the church. Here the intellectual life of the university must reach its highest level of discourse in order to show the unity of all discourse in the Triune God, a unity that always exceeds the discourse itself. As the center of the rational life of the university, the Vice President of Academic Affairs should have ultimate responsibility for chapel in close collaboration with the President. Because students in their general education will have begun to understand the difference between entertainment and truthful homiletic discourses and between therapeutic developmental psychological advice for late adolescents and proper Christian language, the university will free the chaplain to encode the students' lives into the Scriptural narrative rather than seek to make the Scriptures relevant to them.[35] Chapel sermons can provide deeper probing in the difference between the Christian life as a thankful pilgrimage through this world from God to God as a member of Christ's body and a life lived for this age as a member of a liberal democratic society. Chapel can constantly explore the strategies and tactics necessary to share in the world's goods without assimilating into its practices and malformation. Chapel should be the primary location where students learn the Christian craft of plundering the Egyptians.[36]

Scriptural readings shared in common with the church catholic should form the basis of the regular Ministry of the Word that constitutes chapel. The chapel discourse should be structured so as to render intelligible a weekly practice of the Eucharist in which the university is made the church visible to the world through Christ's body and blood, one Body, students, faculty, administration, and staff alike. Chapel should be structured to form the student deeper and deeper into the language of prayer and praise appropriate to the university.

As students approach graduation, special sessions need to be held to explain the difference between the discourse of a university chapel and that of a local congregation. Students, with deeper formation than those without the gift of a habitus from the Christian university, will need to be warned concerning the perils of spiritual pride. Young, energetic, and impulsive, they will need to be instructed in the need for patience and the importance of unity, constancy, and peace for local congregations in order to enhance the witness of the church amid a culture that would make worship a commodity on the local board of ecclesial trade. In this way, the university can sustain a constituency within local churches over time even as the local churches become equipped to sustain a Christian university that seeks to form its students through a Christian habitus.

Third, once encountering the Christian Scriptures in their native environment of the gathering of the church in worship, "general education" Scripture classes can provide instruction in the Scriptural text through exploring the grammar of participation in God's own self-knowledge from Scripture. As already encountered in worship, the professor can explicate the underlying doctrines of Christian revelation in Jesus Christ and the Scriptures' role as a witness to the revelation of God in Jesus—the Christological and ecclesiological end of Scripture. The class should explore the narrative structure of Scripture as it finds its climax in Jesus Christ and the life of the church.

As the texts are creation, not God, the professor can examine the historical formation of the texts as the means of God's providential sanctifying of these texts in accordance with the gospel witness that "salvation comes from the Jews."[37] One class should cover the whole Scriptures, rather than separate classes for the Old Testament or New Testament. Scholars must suspend disciplinary specializations within the Society of Biblical Literature or the American Academy of Religion to study the proper social and political context of this literature in the worship and life of the church through the ages. In this way, the general education curriculum can dissolve the artificial theological divisions between theology and biblical studies and church history. They all provide momentary glimpses into the greater life of the worship and prayer of the church.

Throughout the class, students must discover that faith and reason are not two distinct qualities, but represent a continuum within rationality.[38] As faith gives rise to reason, so reason raises and purifies faith to show its true nature as reason in its culmination in the *Logos*, Jesus Christ, the crucified and risen Lord of all creation, the same *Logos* testified to in the Scriptures.[39] The historical conditions of the production of the text do not annul or confirm their status as Scripture; rather the students can grasp how these texts are taken up and made to be what they truly are when placed into the narrative relations provided by the Rule of Faith within the worship of the church as a witness to the Triune God. The professor must displace a Kantian framework that posits a realm of "pure reason" against faith and revelation, and concepts of faith and revelation that stand outside of reason. Faith does not annul reason, but provides the necessary conditions to see the Scriptural texts for what they really were by what they have become. The class must give a language to what the students have already experienced in chapel, an experience already enriched after their first year General Education class on the university and chapel. The students will have had opportunity to receive a language to accompany the habitus that renders theology—the knowledge of the Triune God as One Unknown—a rational discourse that, in turn, renders intelligible the world in which they live.

By centering the university's general education upon chapel, the university is free to engage in faithful learning, to discover, for instance, that the sciences do not study nature per se, but creation. As creation, God has created that which is other than God's own Being from God's own Being. Thus, creation is both contingent—it has a history—and has been gifted with its own existence with a proper autonomy in and of itself. Thus, theology does not dictate what the biologist discovers in the lab, though it surely may have much to say about what questions are asked, to what end the technology is applied, and from whom the biologist accepts funding.

Placing the worship of God as central in the university also frees faculty to rethink the disciplines, to teach the disciplines shaped by the habitus of the Kantian university, but to teach them not as natural, but as part of rival collectives and thus to maximize the benefit and limit the harm that they can do. The faculty must provide wisdom so as to open the students up to creative tactics to live life in the world as members of local congregations rather than as professionals who have careers. The faculty must help their students avoid falling into idolatry later in life. Faculty and students alike will find the imaginary lines of disciplines dissolving as courses bleed into each other, such as philosophy, literature, theology, and art. Business classes can be taught where profit is a good, but a good in which economic exchanges serve humans rather than humans serving economic exchanges. Management classes become sites, not to produce higher rates of laborer efficiency per se, but to help management efficiency serve the laborer so that the laborer can use the material goods of this world for the glory and worship of God. A unity of teaching and research come together in the ordering of the goods of the human intellect as we find our beginning and end in the God who created us, called forth Israel amid the nations, redeemed us in Jesus Christ, and called us into the church as we await the eschatological renewal of all things in Christ.

A Faithful Habitus for Truthful Learning within the University

Returning to the origins of the university in the monastic transformation of the medieval schools through re-centering the university around worship allows us to have formed in us and our students a habitus of Wisdom, a means of ordering goods in light of the Good that is God amid a world that would pull us into an agonistic struggle between hegemony and resistance. It will take the faithfulness of the martyrs, witnesses who did not lose confidence in the face of receiving the full brunt of violence for refusing to play by the faith, the allegiances of the society around them.[40]

Perhaps the deep struggles in the life of the universities around us should give us strength, even as we work outside these corridors of wealth, power, and influence. It is generally agreed that such universities in the United States have lost intelligibility as institutions other than providing a means of economic exchanges, student credentialing for recognition and financial wealth, and professorial questing for professional status. Without theology, its founding discourse and the life of the church to sustain it, it is not apparent that the university can sustain a coherent life and continue its drift into irrelevancy. It may be, as Stanley Hauerwas has recently argued, that the university needs theology to be saved from the arbitrary, irrational powers of the marketplace.[41]

Such struggles within the contemporary university with its Kantian genealogy should not surprise us. The formation of the habitus necessary to sustain theological discourse was a foundation of the Western university, and may provide a *sine qua non* of its existence over time. We must remember our history:

> the university originated, not out of acquiescence to the demands for more specialized and practical learning, but out of resistance to these pressures. The university was a victory, if never a complete one, for a higher educational ideal. The examination of how this important victory was achieved might help to answer the questions of why the university has survived for so long and what are the most serious threats to its future.[42]

The formation of a habitus necessary to sustain theological discourse seems to lie at the center of this victory. If so, its recovery in institutions could provide a gift to sustain such a discourse until other universities find it or are radically transformed by different social and economic conditions into a vestige of a new type of institution that leaves the university behind. Our deepest relevance may lie in our patience, in our willingness to be utterly irrelevant in our main task of forming a habitus of worship in our students—and allowing the Holy Spirit to bring forth one in us—that renders theology intelligible as a discourse of knowledge.

Chapter 8 Notes

1. The categories of "encyclopaedia" and "genealogy" are taken from Alasdair MacIntyre, *Three Rival Versions of Moral Enquiry:Encyclopaedia, Genealogy, and Tradition* (Notre Dame, IN: University of Notre Dame Press, 1990). Bruno Latour speaks of the same configuration in his analysis of "the modern constitution" in *We Have Never Been Modern* (Cambridge, MA: Harvard University Press, 1993), 13-48.

2. MacIntyre, *Three Rival Versions*, 42.

3. See William James, *Pragmatism, a New Name for Some Old Ways of Thinking* (New York: Longmans, Green, and Co., 1922), 54-55.

4. MacIntyre, *Three Rival Versions*, 42.

5. Thomas Albert Howard, *Protestant Theology and the Making of the Modern German University* (Oxford: Oxford University Press, 2006), 123.

6. Jacques Derrida, "Mochlos; or, The Conflict of the Faculties" in *Logomachia: The Conflict of the Faculties,* ed. Richard Rand (Lincoln, NE: University of Nebraska Press, 1992), 6.

7. Immanuel Kant, "The Conflict of the Faculties," in *Religion and Rational Theology*, ed. Allen Wood and George Di Giovanni (Cambridge: Cambridge University Press, 1996), 250.

8. Kant, "The Conflict of the Faculty," 256.

9. Ibid., 285.

10. Howard, *Protestant Theology*, 22.

11. Kant, "The Conflict of the Faculty," 287.

12. Ibid., 264.

13. Ibid., 267.

14. Ibid.

15. Derrida, "Mochlos," 11-12.

16. Pierre Bourdieu, *Outline of a Theory of Practice*, trans. Richard Nice (Cambridge: Cambridge University Press, 1977), 72.

17. Ibid., 78.

18. Ibid., 72.

19. Derrida, "Mochlos," 18.

20. Talal Asad, *Genealogies of Religion: Discipline and Reasons of Power in Christianity and Islam* (Baltimore: Johns Hopkins University Press, 1993), 204.

21. See Robert Bellah, et al., *Habits of the Heart: Individualism and Commitment in American Life* (Berkeley, CA: University of California Press, 1985), 46-51.

22. Alasdair MacIntyre, *After Virtue: A Study in Moral Theory* (Notre Dame, IN: University of Notre Dame Press, 1981), 30.

23. Such is the description of Derrida's politics in Richard Rand, "Preface" in *Logomachia*, ix.

24. See Andrew Abbott, *The System of Professions: An Essay on the Division of Expert Labor* (Chicago: University of Chicago Press, 1988).

25. One finds here the network that has constructed the new "developmental stage" of "emerging adulthood." See Jeffrey Jensen Arnett, *Emerging Adulthood: The Winding Road from the Late Teens Through the Twenties* (Oxford: Oxford University Press, 2004).

26. See Christian Smith and Melina Lundquist Denton, *Soul Searching: The Religious Lives of American Teenagers* (Oxford: Oxford University Press, 2005), 162-71, especially 165.

27. See Karl Barth, "The Task of Prolegomena to Dogmatics," *Church Dogmatics 1.1: The Doctrine of the Word of God* (trans. G. T. Thomson; Edinburgh: T. & T. Clark, 1936), 26-47.

28. Derrida, "Mochlos," 29-30.

29. See David M. Burrell "Religion and the University," *CrossCurrents* (Summer 2006), www.crosscurrents.org/burrellsummer2006.pdf.

30. John Milbank, "The Conflict of the Faculties: Theology and the Economy of the Sciences," in *Faithfulness and Fortitude: Conversations with the Theological Ethics of Stanley Hauerwas*, ed. Mark Nation and Samuel Wells (London: T & T Clark, 2000), 45.

31. See Stephen Ferruolo, *The Origins of University: The Schools of Paris and Their Critics, 1100-1215* (Stanford, CA: Stanford University Press, 1985).

32. For similar proposals, see Gavin D'Costa, "Why Theologians Must Pray for Release from Exile," in *Theology in the Public Square: Church, Academy and Nation*, Challenges in Contemporary Theology (Oxford: Blackwell Publishing, 2005), 112-44, and James K. A. Smith, *Desiring the Kingdom: Worship, Worldview, and Cultural Formation*, Cultural Liturgies, vol. 1 (Grand Rapids, MI: Baker Academic, 2009).

33. See Jean LeClercq, OSB, *The Love of Learning and Desire for God: A Study of Monastic Culture* (New York: Fordham University Press, 1982). See also Mark A. Noll, *Jesus Christ and the Life of the Mind* (Grand Rapids, MI: Eerdmans, 2011).

34. See Edward Yarnold, SJ, *The Awe-Inspiring Rites of Initiation: The Origins of the R.C.I.A.*, 2nd edition (Edinburgh: T. & T. Clark, 1994). See also Paul F. Bradshaw, Maxwell E. Johnson, and L. Edward Phillips, *The Apostolic Tradition*, Hermeneia (Minneapolis: Fortress Press, 2002), 82-151.

35. See John W. Wright, *Telling God's Story: Narrative Preaching for Christian Formation* (Downers Grove, IL: IVP Academic, 2007).

36. See Henri de Lubac, *Medieval Exegesis. Vol. 1: The Four Senses of Scripture*, trans. Mark Sebanc; Ressourcement: Retrieval and Renewal in Catholic Thought (Grand Rapid, MI: Eerdmans , 1998), 211-24.

37. See John Webster, *Holy Scripture: A Dogmatic Sketch*, Current Issues in Theology (Cambridge: Cambridge University Press, 2003).

38. See the excellent collection in Paul J. Griffiths and Reinhard Hütter, eds., *Reasons and the Reasons of Faith*, Theology for the Twenty-First Century (New York: T & T. Clark, 2005); Laurence Paul Hemming and Susan Frank Parsons, eds., *Restoring Faith in Reason: A New Translation of the Encyclical* Faith and Reason *of Pope John Paul II, Together with a Commentary and Discussion*, Faith in Reason (Notre Dame, IN: University of Notre Dame Press, 2002); and Conor Cunningham and Peter Candler, eds., *The Grandeur of Reason: Religion, Tradition, and Universalism*, Veritas Series (London: SCM Press, 2009).

39. See David L. Schindler, "Introduction: Grace and the Form of Nature and Culture" in *Catholicism and Secularization in America: Essays on Nature, Grace, and Culture*, ed. David L. Schindler (Huntington, IN: Our Sunday Visitor Publishing Division, 1990), 10-30.

40. See Michael L. Budde and Karen Scott, eds., *Witness of the Body: The Past, Present, and Future of Christian Martyrdom* (Grand Rapids, MI: Eerdmans , 2011).

41. Stanley Hauerwas, "The Pathos of the University: The Case of Stanley Fish," in *The State of the University: Academic Knowledges and the Knowledge of God*, Illuminations: Theory and Religion (Oxford: Blackwell Publishing, 2007), 76-91.

42. Ferruolo, *The Origins of University*, 7-8.

CONCLUSION

Jerry Pattengale

When we began this journey to reevaluate the current implications of integration, we were aware of the topic's complexity and the possibility of being relegated to another trite discussion. But as these chapters have revealed, several new directions are manifest in Christian higher education, along with clear challenges for new directions. And suffice it to say that this text's authors are thinkers of the caliber not given to trite matters.

The original Reformed notion of integration has indeed stretched far beyond its anticipated use, and is increasingly multi-disciplinary. And likewise, the practice of thoughtful integration is one steeped in deeper thinking. In *Jesus Christ and the Life of the Mind,* Mark Noll emphases that it's counterintuitive for evangelicals not to be given to scholarship, and that those taking seriously the underpinning person and attributes of Christ will indeed pursue deeper truths.

In this vein, David Lyle Jeffrey reveals the charge of scholars like Matthew Arnold, T. S. Eliot, and C. S. Lewis to give the Bible its due place in the curriculum, though the latter two argued for the rightful place of transcendent imagination. Conversely, the majority of Literature scholars separated the Bible from its ontological origins, which led to incoherence. Jeffrey argues that the main concern for the future is the preservation of cultural history, and the primary task that of keeping great works (especially the canonical authors) alive and relevant. The Christian liberal arts institutions must keep their nerve to persist in this regard, even if they are perceived as unfashionable. The essence of a liberal arts education, and the precursor to any hope of integrating faith and learning, is for these colleges unabashedly and passionately to teach the principles and model the practices of reading with discernment—with the great texts as objective standards of inquiry.

In the academy at large, and ironically led by MLA members, the traditionally text-heavy disciplines are shifting the emphasis from the author and text to the reader. While they are de-valuing "weaving" and the substance of the texts, Christian universities need more than ever to reject this "leveling" process and champion their classics—built around and in conversation with the Bible.

In history evangelical scholars need to worry about this leveling trend; this in addition to navigating the ongoing tension between those in the academy suspicious of scholars from faith traditions, and those within the faith tradition who unduly chastise other Christians for imbibing scholarly standards and endorsing methodological naturalism. Timothy Larsen's discussion of this dynamic is masterful, including his charge to keep the roles of academic historians separate from those of ministers and prophets. He also points to the easy congruence of one's faith informing sound scholarship—from the choice of subject matter to the parameters of a study (such as including the remarkable preaching dynamic of Pankhurst's career). Likewise, the decision to leave room for God's working and sincere spiritual interests among the motivations and answers.

Just as Larsen challenges Christian historians to be the best at their profession— telling the most compelling stories with the best evidence, presentation, and interpretations—we need to mentor our students in all academic divisions to do the same. At the core of the integration of faith and learning is integrity to both.

John Wright calls for the same level of scholarly integrity in theological disciplines, and cautions Christian universities against either a blind or misinformed Kantian structure. In this regard, one would do well to read the late Bill Placher's *Triune God* alongside Wright's chapter, championing theology as the queen of the sciences and also reveling in the mystery of meanings. Like this volume's chapter on philosophy, Wright finds it alarming that divine revelation, in any of its perceived forms, is relegated by the nation-state to the periphery of any discussion of knowledge. He argues that "The university habituates students into a system that sees the state, not the church, as significant for human life and activity. Such a habitus renders theology unintelligible."

So what is a possible answer to this bleak position for theologians? Wright's short answer is to return theology to being more about "truth" than "therapy." Like James K. A. Smith, Wright calls us to recognize the formative value of the language of prayer and worship. His bold outline places the chapel and worship as the university's fulcrum for both credit-bearing and student development strategies. Wright and Jamie Smith both follow Stanley Hauerwas' clarion call for Christian colleges to remember their key reason for existence—to know more about God's love.[1]

In sociology, Larsen's proposed integrity involves remembering the past while charting the future. The influence of religious ideas and theological motifs on the founding of sociology are key factors in the road to integration, especially in an era in the academy marked with a "fluidity of disciplinary boundaries." Although the particular sociology/theology divide remains pronounced, Christian sociologists have a strong starting point in recognizing their historic place within their discipline and the academy.

Perhaps no discipline has received more attention during the rise of postmodernism than philosophy, and especially its bearing on religious thought and scholarship. As this text is going to press, Adam Kirsch, senior editor of *The New Republic,* criticizes the authors of the liberal *The Bible Now.* He doesn't condemn their conclusions (which he basically endorses) but their perceived need to reconcile anything with ancient texts, such as the Bible. He cites Immanuel Kant in calling them "immature" for their "lack of resolve and courage to use it [their understanding] without guidance from another."[2]

While this scenario of scholarly exchange seems bleak for the discipline of Christian philosophy, James K. A. Smith sees it quite differently. He proposes a radical approach that combines the biblical narrative's "thickness" with Christian worship's "social imaginary" (a term adapted from Charles Taylor). Given Kirsch's condemnation of scholars' desire to consult the biblical texts, any hope of improving a Christian scholar's footing in the secular academy will indeed need to be radical—one Smith calls "unapologetics." Conversely, places like Cape Cod's Church of the Transfiguration (and its artistic monastic community) will likely applaud Smith's emphasis on our liturgical underpinnings.

Smith's challenge to uproot current practices, especially the very reliance on integration and worldview models, seems to contrast with Timothy Larsen's lucid notions in this volume. What Larsen calls excellence and integrity, Smith lumps with syncretism. Whereas Larsen challenges Christian scholars to address important questions, Smith seems to imply that this is merely grafting to a secularist's model. Smith's "confessional realism" means that we all come to the table from formative heritages that inform our work. We all, secular and otherwise, apply faith in some manner. The nomenclature Smith is espousing here is indeed radical. And, many terms might pass for the very terms he's challenging. What worldview institutes are calling "worldviews" have many of the components in Smith's "revelation" category, and likewise in the very notion of "confessional."

It's not clear in Smith's view how a Christian scholar would respond to Kirsch's disdain for consulting ancient texts, the very texts that prompt Smith passion for this issue. However, given Smith's impressive corpus, it's fitting that we consider such options in a work entitled "Beyond Integration." At the least, Smith articulates well the experiential role in our understanding, and the case for the full-sensory description of what we "understand." The prescription for Christian scholarship, as in the Kirsch challenge, will not be as easy.

The notion of scholars as affective animals with a social imaginary influencing their pre-theoretical understanding (and ultimately their theories) is obviously an aspect of this larger question of integration intersecting with psychology, sociology, theology, and a host of disciplines. Smith would be pleased with the notions that all disciplines would consider this seriously, become more entrenched in biblical foundations, and develop habits of seeing ("attuned" to Christian concerns).

In this volume, Smith's views find a welcome intersection with psychology. Mary Stewart Van Leeuwen and Jade Avelis immediately endorse the notion that "all research is autobiography" and that there are no "views from nowhere." As Smith argues, scholars are indeed affective and all bring some aspect of faith to the discussion. The target of our worship, gods of any type, direct our lives and yes, our research. Religion's prominence in psychological studies is a manifestation of this postmodern (post-empiricist) development.

"Critical Realism" may indeed be a middle ground in psychology that will allow Christian thinking an engaging place in the academy. Van Leeuwen and Avelis' argument is appealing for a system that respects the various structures of our perceptions while respecting their limits in imposing a structure on reality. They also highlight the importance of funding internships in orthodox Christian programs for promising graduate students at top programs, much like the Blackstone program for the Alliance Defense Fund. These funded options are limited, and perhaps other venues like post-doc programs can facilitate similar objectives.

The exchange between science and faith remains complex, with many scholars adamantly espousing the conflict view, finding the two views perpetually and irrevocable at odds. Another issue remains the gap between popular misperceptions about science and actual science, and Christian colleges should help to narrow this divide. And we are all aware of the many factions among Christian scholars, from the national science organizations to the more focused groups like BioLogos.

Edward Davis emphasizes the need for the humanistic study of the sciences, whether in an academic major or in targeted classes, and the hiring of faculty members so prepared. He also underscores the need to teach many scientific models and allow students (and faculty) to decide their veracity. The landscape has radically changed since the polarized time of William Jennings Bryan; today leading orthodox Christian scientists like John Polkinghorne and Francis Collins also endorse evolutionary models.

Davis's chapter on science and faith does not champion the very notions that preoccupy the chapters by Smith and Van Leeuwen—with their emphasis on social imaginary and critical realism. Instead, his more traditional approach to a way forward, as with Larsen's endorsement of research integrity, is itself revealing. That is, while some Christian institutions of higher learning have already experienced pronounced steps by their scholars of movement beyond the original Reformed model of integration, the face of a new model is still in the making. Whether a new model ever gains the cohesive synergism as the original one is perhaps an entertaining question, but what we've learned in this volume is that regardless of any formal outline, diagram, or theory, it appears that the affective aspect of being human will factor more significantly in the quest to know more fully God's love.

Conclusion Notes

1. Jerry Pattengale, "What Are Universities For? The Contested Terrain of Moral Education," *Books and Culture,* review of Elizabeth Kiss and J. Peter Euben, editors, *Debating Moral Education: Rethinking the Role of the Modern University* (Duke University Press, 2010).

2. Adam Kirsch, "Progressive Inversions," *The New Republic* (15 July 2011).

EPILOGUE

Henry L. Smith
President, Indiana Wesleyan University

This volume points us down a path that is certainly in tune with the missions of most evangelical institutions, and likely Christian universities of various stripes.

There is a unity in the mélange of suggestions in this volume. Though some appear in tension, with Jamie Smith's the most *radical* regardless of whether we use the traditional or the "Smith" rendition of the term. But if there is a paradigm shift in the making, as Smith champions, we'll all need to continue a robust conversation.

Jamie's lectures at Indiana Wesleyan University brought large crowds and prompted a shift to much larger facilities. The response seemed to indicate the timeliness of his questions as well as his pro-vocative answers. The other lectures in this series (and in turn, many of these book chapters) were also refreshingly engaging. If such reception is indicative of the Christian community's interest in notions of moving beyond the original integration model, then a new paradigm is indeed in the making.

Like the editors of this book, and as a board member of the Council of Christian Colleges and Universities, I resonate with the notion attrib-uted to Stanley Hauerwas that in the end our educational purpose is about knowing more fully God and his love. And, as a president who has given decades to serving accrediting bodies, I believe that as private institutions we can have this focus while maintaining both self-imposed and external standards of excellence. We continue to build curricula, programs, and financial models around this purposeful pursuit, and as administrators and professors we walk away from this volume encouraged to let our philosophy drive the logistics of our planning and building.

Contributors

Jade Avelis is a Ph.D. student in sociology at the University of Notre Dame. A recipient of a Lilly Endowment scholarship and a 2008 *magna cum laude* graduate of the John Wesley Honors College at Indiana Wesleyan University, Jade's research interests include gender, marriage and family, religion, social psychology, and work-nonwork balance.

Edward B. Davis (Ph.D., Indiana University) is Professor of the History of Science at Messiah College (Grantham, PA) and Director of the Central Pennsylvania Forum for Religion and Science. With Michael Hunter, Dr. Davis edited *The Works of Robert Boyle*, 14 vols. (Pickering & Chatto, 1999-2000), and a separate edition of Boyle's subtle treatise on God and nature, *A Free Enquiry into the Vulgarly Received Notion of Nature* (Cambridge University Press, 1996). Author of dozens of articles about the history of Christianity and science in early modern Europe and the United States, his study of modern Jonah stories was featured on two BBC radio programs. His current research, supported by the National Science Foundation and the John Templeton Foundation, examines the religious activities and beliefs of prominent American scientists from the period between the two world wars.

David Lyle Jeffrey (Ph.D., Princeton University) is Distinguished Professor of Literature & Humanities in the Honors Program at Baylor University. He is also Professor Emeritus of English Literature at the University of Ottawa and Guest Professor at Peking University (Beijing). The former Associate Provost and Provost at Baylor, David is the general editor and co-author of *A Dictionary of Biblical Tradition in English Literature*. Among his other books are *The Early English Lyric and Franciscan Spirituality, By Things Seen: Reference and Recognition in Medieval Thought, Chaucer and Scriptural Tradition, English Spirituality in the Age of Wesley, The Law of Love: English Spirituality in the Age of Wyclif, People of the Book: Christian Identity and Literary Culture, House of the Interpreter: Reading Scripture, Reading Culture,* and with Gregory Maillet, *Christianity and Literature: Philosophical Foundations and Critical Practice.*

Timothy Larsen (Ph.D., University of Stirling) is the Carolyn and Fred McManis Professor of Christian Thought, Wheaton College (Illinois), where he is also Director of the faculty development Faith and Learning Program. He is a Fellow of the Royal Historical Society, has been a Visiting Fellow in History, Trinity College, Cambridge University, and he was elected a Visiting Fellow in History, All Souls College, Oxford University, for 2012. Tim is a Contributing Editor for *Books & Culture* and has edited a range of volumes including the *Biographical Dictionary of Evangelicals* and the *Cambridge Companion to Evangelical Theology*. His single-authored volumes include *Crisis of Doubt: Honest Faith in Nineteenth-Century England*, *Contested Christianity: The Political and Social Contexts of Victorian Theology*, *Friends of Religious Equality: Nonconformist Politics in Mid-Victorian England*, *Christabel Pankhurst: Fundamentalism and Feminism in Coalition*, and most recently, *A People of One Book: The Bible and the Victorians*.

Jerry Pattengale (Ph.D., Miami University-Ohio) serves as the director of the Green Scholars Initiative. He also is the Assistant Provost for Public Engagement at Indiana Wesleyan University, a Senior Fellow at the Sagamore Institute, a Research Scholar at Gordon-Conwell Theological Seminary, Research Associate at Tyndale House, University of Cambridge, and a Distinguished Senior Fellow at Baylor University's Institute for Studies of Religion. He speaks nationally in various venues and on a wide range of college campuses. Jerry's recent books and projects include: *Why I Teach* and *The Purpose-Guided Student* (McGraw-Hill, 2009, 2010), *Helping Sophomores Succeed* (Jossey-Bass, 2010), *What Faculty Members Need to Know about Retention* (Magna Publications, 2011), *Taking Every Thought Captive* (Abilene Christian University Press, 2011), *Biblical Evidence* (Indiana Wesleyan University Press, 2011), and *The Passages Film Series* (12 vols. [A1], Green Scholars Initiative, 2011). He has earned various teaching and educational awards, including "The National Student Advocate Award" from the University of South Carolina's National Resource Center and a National Endowment for the Humanities award to Isthmia, Greece. He is the Associate Publisher for *Christian Scholar's Review*.

Todd C. Ream (Ph.D., Pennsylvania State University) is the Senior Scholar for Faith and Scholarship and an Associate Professor of

Humanities in the John Wesley Honors College at Indiana Wesleyan University. He also serves as a Research Fellow with the Institute for Studies of Religion at Baylor University. Todd is the author of *Christian Faith and Scholarship: An Exploration of Contemporary Developments* (with Perry L. Glanzer, Jossey-Bass, 2007), *Christianity and Moral Identity in Higher Education* (with Perry L. Glanzer, Palgrave Macmillan, 2009), and *A Parent's Guide to the Christian College: Supporting Your Child's Mind and Spirit During the College Years* (with Timothy W. Herrmann and C. Skip Trudeau, Abilene Christian University Press, 2011). He also serves as the Book Review Editor (with Perry L. Glanzer) for *Christian Scholar's Review*.

David L. Riggs (D.Phil., Oxford University) is Associate Professor of Humanities and Executive Director of the John Wesley Honors College at Indiana Wesleyan University. David's research focuses primarily on the religious world of late antiquity. He is preparing a manuscript on the cultic life of late-antique North Africa for Oxford University Press (*Divine Patronage in Late Antique North Africa*). He is also engaged in a collaborative research project (with Christopher Bounds and a group of John Wesley Honors College students) exploring patristic conceptions of "grace" in light of Graeco-Roman models of patronage. Additionally, David is co-editing (with Stan Rosenberg) a monograph for the National Collegiate Honors Council entitled *Seeking the Soul of Excellence: Developing Spirituality in Honors Education*.

Jeanne Heffernan Schindler (Ph.D., University of Notre Dame) is Assistant Professor in the Department of Humanities and Affiliate Professor in the School of Law at Villanova University. Her interests are interdisciplinary, integrating philosophy, theology, and political science. She has published in such areas as Catholic social thought, democratic theory, moral theology, and faith and learning. Her most recent major publication is an edited volume on *Christianity and Civil Society: Catholic and Neo-Calvinist Perspectives* (Lexington Books, 2008). With her husband, D. C. Schindler, she is currently editing an anthology of essays by the contemporary German Catholic philosopher, Robert Spaemann. Her next book-length project will explore the concept of freedom at work in American jurisprudence.

John A. Schmalzbauer (Ph.D., Princeton University) is Associate Professor and holds the Blanche Gorman Strong Chair in Protestant Studies at Missouri State University. His teaching and research focus on the role of Protestantism in American society and he is especially interested in the role of religion in popular culture, Protestant evangelicalism, American Catholicism, and the place of religion in American higher education. In recent years, his courses have also focused on religion in the Ozarks. His book, *People of Faith: Religious Conviction in American Journalism and Higher Education,* explores the role of religion in the careers of forty prominent journalists and academics. John is also currently writing a book on the return of religion on campus with Kathleen Mahoney.

Henry L. Smith (Ph.D., Ohio State University) is the eighth President of Indiana Wesleyan University. He came to IWU in the summer of 2004, as IWU's first executive vice president, and assumed the IWU presidency on July 1, 2006. Having devoted his professional life to Christian higher education, he has served as a professor, a director of campus radio stations, a graduate dean, an academic vice president, an executive vice president and now president. He was the dean of the graduate school at Olivet Nazarene University and the provost and chief academic officer at Mount Vernon Nazarene University before coming to Indiana Wesleyan University. In addition to his administrative duties, Henry has served as a peer reviewer for the Higher Learning Commission and a board member for the Council for Christian Colleges and Universities.

James K. A. Smith (Ph.D., Villanova University) is Professor of Philosophy and Adjunct Professor of Congregational and Ministry Studies at Calvin College. He also serves as a Senior Fellow for the Collosian Forum on Faith, Science, and Culture. His interests reside at the intersection of philosophy, theology, and cultural criticism. The author or editor of over fifteen books, some of his most recent works include *Teaching and Christian Practices: Reshaping Faith and Learning* (co-edited with David I. Smith), *Letters to a Young Calvinist: An Invitation to the Reformed Tradition, Speaking in Tongues: Pentecostal Contributions to Christian Philosophy,* and *Desiring the Kingdom: Worship, Worldview,* *and Cultural Formation*. He is currently at work on the sequel to *Desiring the Kingdom* and a short introduction to Charles Taylor's *A Secular Age*.

Mary Stewart Van Leeuwen (Ph.D., Northwestern University) is Professor of Psychology and Chair of the Department of Psychology at Eastern University. A leading voice among evangelicals in terms of understandings of gender, she is the author of a number of books including *The Person in Psychology after Eden, Gender and Grace: Love, Work, and Parenting in a Changing World, My Brother's Keeper: What the Social Sciences Do (and Don't) Tell Us About Masculinity*, and *A Sword Between the Sexes: C. S. Lewis and the Gender Debates*.

John W. Wright (Ph.D., University of Notre Dame) is Professor of Theology and Christian Scriptures at Point Loma Nazarene University and Senior Pastor of The Church of the Nazarene, Mid-City English. He is the author or editor of a number of books including *Telling God's Story: Narrative Preaching for Christian Formation, Conflicting Allegiances: The Church-Based University in a Liberal Democratic Society* (edited with Michael L. Budde), and *Postliberal Theology and the Church Catholic: Conversations with George Lindbeck, David Burrell, and Stanley Hauerwas*. He also maintains a popular blog at http://www.pastor-johnwright.org/.

INDEX OF SUBJECTS AND AUTHORS

by Sheri Klouda
Associate Professor of Biblical Studies and Hebrew
Taylor University